THE SHAMANIC ODYSSEY

"The authors' exploration of the shamanic, indigenous characteristics of Odysseus's journey through the ancient otherworld of divine powers is a noteworthy new contribution to the field of Classics. In particular, their reading of the Odysseus and the Cyclops episode in light of the encounter between the indigenous peoples of the Americas and the 'civilized' European conquistadores opens marvelous new possibilities for understanding the mind of Homeric man."

CARL A. P. RUCK, PH.D., PROFESSOR OF CLASSICAL STUDIES AT BOSTON UNIVERSITY AND COAUTHOR OF *THE ROAD TO ELEUSIS*

"A unique and insightful comparative look at the *Odyssey* and the South American shamanic tradition—highly recommended!"

MARK PLOTKIN, AUTHOR OF *THE SHAMAN'S APPRENTICE* AND *MEDICINE QUEST*

"Tindall and Bustos do more than remind us of a world celebrated by visionaries—from Homer to Shakespeare to Tolkien to indigenous shamans—a world where the old gods walked with us and the animals taught us how to live and the plants healed us. They take us there."

STEVE WALKER, PH.D., PROFESSOR AT BYU COLLEGE OF HUMANITIES AND AUTHOR OF *THE POWER OF TOLKIEN'S PROSE*

"Placing the story firmly in a shamanic context—including touching upon sacred psychoactive plants, ancient bardic song, vision quest, and the creative mythology of Middle earth—the authors present us with a Homer who is an indigenous singer of healing song. Tindall and Bustos have a truly comprehensive vision, a striking depth of knowledge, a scholar's love of language, and a compelling storyteller's way of tying together the many threads. A significant and hugely enjoyable book."

STEPHAN V. BEYER, AUTHOR OF *SINGING TO THE PLANTS*

"*The Shamanic Odyssey* is a brilliant book! The authors explore wildness in the form of plant spirits, indigenous peoples, and ancient roots of deep knowledge. They illustrate what one meets on a shamanic quest, whether mythic, collective, or individual. The treatment is erudite, illuminating, and deeply insightful."

KATHLEEN HARRISON, M.A., ETHNOBOTANIST

THE SHAMANIC ODYSSEY

Homer, Tolkien, and the Visionary Experience

Robert Tindall

with Susana Bustos, Ph.D.

Park Street Press
Rochester, Vermont • Toronto, Canada

Park Street Press
One Park Street
Rochester, Vermont 05767
www.ParkStPress.com

Text stock is SFI certified

Park Street Press is a division of Inner Traditions International

Library of Congress Cataloging-in-Publication Data

Tindall, Robert.
  The shamanic odyssey : Homer, Tolkien, and the visionary experience / Robert Tindall with Susana Bustos, Ph.D.
      p. cm.
  Includes bibliographical references and index.
  Summary: "Reveals the striking parallels between indigenous cultures of the Americas and the ancient Homeric world as well as Tolkien's Middle Earth"— Provided by publisher.
  ISBN 978-1-59477-396-9 (pbk.) — ISBN 978-1-59477-501-7 (e-book)
  1. Shamanism. 2. Shamanism in literature. I. Bustos, Susana. II. Title.
GN475.8.T56 2012
201'.44—dc23
                                                                    2012014068

Printed and bound in the United States by Lake Book Manufacturing, Inc. The text stock is SFI certified. The Sustainable Forestry Initiative® program promotes sustainable forest management.

10 9 8 7 6 5 4 3 2 1

Text design by Jack Nichols and layout by Brian Boynton
This book was typeset in Garamond Premier Pro with OPTI Benjie Modern, Thonburi, and Gill Sans as display typefaces

To send correspondence to the authors of this book, mail a first-class letter to the authors c/o Inner Traditions • Bear & Company, One Park Street, Rochester, VT 05767, and we will forward the communication, or visit the authors' website at **www.roamingthemind.com**.

For our daughter Maitreya, Virgencita Ikunanta,
who illuminates our way

Are most of the allegorized, dramatized, literalized, sanitized, boring, overly historified rituals and written stories only jealously guarded fragments of a pushed-aside indigenous intactness which all people, in this increasingly displaced world, have hidden somewhere in their bones as an unremembered legacy in which an intact living story still waits to come into view?

MARTÍN PRECHTEL

Upon arriving in Byzantium, Hierocles, the fifth-century Alexandrian philosopher, seems to have offended certain Christians and was therefore whipped in the presence of the Christian magistrate. Taking some of his blood in the cup of his hand, Hierocles sprinkled the judge with it, quoting these lines from the Odyssey: "Cyclops, since human flesh is thy delight, Now drink this wine."

KENNETH SYLVAN GUTHRIE

CONTENTS

FOREWORD

My dad taught Latin. I was raised on the classics. Homer's epic poem, the *Odyssey*, was bedtime reading in our house.

When a Shuar shaman, deep in the Amazon, saved my life not long after I graduated from college, he demanded that I repay him by becoming his apprentice. "It will be a tough journey," he warned, "but you'll connect with sacred plants and powerful spirit guides . . . just like Etsaa." His description of the adventures of this legendary rain forest hero astounded me. Etsaa so resembled Odysseus that I puzzled over how two cultures so far removed in time and space could share such similar myths.

Later, as an economic hit man, I traveled the world, coercing governments to subjugate their people to a new form of empire led by multinational corporations. During long flights I re-read Homer. I was struck by how little we humans have changed. We had traded sailing ships for airplanes and swords for AK-47s, but we were still hell-bent on exploiting others. I knew that Odysseus would admire the wily tricks-of-trade—the Trojan horses—I and my cohorts employed to conquer other lands.

So, was Odysseus Western literature's first full portrait of a practicing shaman and shapeshifter? What about Odysseus, that ancient Greek raider of cities, as Western literature's first economic hit man?

Sound implausible? All I can say is: "Read on!" Prepare to be amazed by the confluence of ancient and indigenous ways with ruthless modern capitalism, as realized in the character of Odysseus. You may even find yourself agreeing with Tindall and Bustos that the origin of our current global financial meltdown is far older than contemporary predatory capitalism—it can be found in Odysseus's *dolos,* his renowned spirit of trickery and cunning deception.

The Shamanic Odyssey is more than just an exploration of ancient texts, native cultures, and shamanic practices. Like the bards of old, Tindall and Bustos sing the *Odyssey* for our time; this modern version is a warning for a world threatened with ecological collapse and economic injustice. The prophetic voices of our indigenous relatives—the Shuar, Hopi, Kogi, Quechua, Maya, and so many others—have now penetrated the iron bubble of our exploitative society; they expose the causes of its likely collapse. Their voices remind us of our humble, and probably brief, span on this glorious planet. The message we are advised to hear in the *Odyssey* is one that calls us to reconciliation with and respect for the remaining indigenous cultures. Even as I write these words, Wirakuta, the ancient site of pilgrimage for the Huichol peoples of Northern Mexico, is threatened by corporate raiders who seek to enter the sacred ground and strip mine it. The message that echoes through the ages urges us to protect those lands and the cultures that have honored them for millennia.

Tindall and Bustos demonstrate that the *Odyssey*'s oral tradition summons us to heal the break with our own native self, with the indigenous experience of a vital, meaningful cosmos—the ultimate resolution to rapacious capitalism. We do not need to live in oblivion, cut off from the voices of our ancestors and wild nature. As a *nostos,* a homecoming song, the *Odyssey* can call us back again—to a home we recognize and our offspring will seek to inhabit.

JOHN PERKINS

John Perkins is a former economic advisor to the World Bank, UN, IMF, Fortune 500 corporations, and countries in Africa, Asia, Latin America, and the Middle East. He is the author of *Confessions of an Economic Hit Man, The Secret History of the American Empire,* and *Hoodwinked,* a blueprint for a new form of global economics. He is a founder and board member of Dream Change and the Pachamama Alliance, nonprofit organizations devoted to establishing a world our children will want to inherit.

ACKNOWLEDGMENTS

When the Condor of the south flies with the Eagle of
the north, a new day for Earth will awaken!

An indigenous prophecy

I have always felt an affinity with the *amanuensis,* that little figure seen
illustrated in the margins of medieval books. Head cocked, quill poised
over blank manuscript on writing table before him, he listens intently,
ready to faithfully transcribe. I admired his single-minded devotion to the
Word, to capturing and preserving the oral tradition flourishing around
him. His austere craft spoke to a quiet aspiration in my own heart: to
record beautiful things heard in a fitting way.

This book is an outcome of that desire. *The Shamanic Odyssey* was
born and nourished as I sat listening in malocas and tipis, participating
within the indigenous medicinal traditions of the South American jungle
and the North American desert. Like the prophecy of the eagle and condor, in its own way it marks the confluence of two cultural streams in the
persons of two remarkable healers, Juan Flores and Bob Boyll.

Maestro *curandero* Juan Flores Salazar is the founder of
Mayantuyacu, a center for traditional medicine in Pucallpa, Peru, who
has shared the riches of the *vegetalista* tradition of the Amazon with us

for many years now. Unstinting in his hospitality, humor, and wonder for the plants and many other beings of the rain forest, Juan has, *poco a poco,* revealed the native, vital cosmovision that underlies his work to us.

Roadman Bob Boyll, his wife Ann Rosencranz, and members of the Native American Church have prayed with us for our daughter Maitreya in the heart of near-tornado conditions, and with hearts of great kindness have guided us along the peyote way of the Plains Indians. Bob and Ann, as medicine folk of European background, are rare critters, even cultural treasures. Their lives, and those of other Euro-American members of the NAC, demonstrate the possibility of rediscovering and walking on indigenous paths once again. Montrese and Anders, Jaguar, Nick and Lisa, and other NAC members have also made significant contributions to this book.

Tom Walsh of the comparative literature and Daniel Melia of the Celtic studies programs at U.C. Berkeley have offered valuable feedback on this manuscript and deepened my understanding of the ancient Greek and Celtic worlds.

Phan Tu Quynh, our illustrator, has worked with sensitivity and diligence to render the indigenous and ancient art reproduced in this book. J. P. Harpignes, Joanna Reichhold, Bob Boyll, Richard Koenig, Jeff Jenkins (Pluma Blanco), Lia Gatey, Robert Forte, David Teachout, Adine Gavazzi, China Galland, Brian Anderson, and others have scrutinized and enriched this manuscript in countless ways.

Most of all, however, I want to acknowledge my coauthor and wife, Susana, who has made crucial contributions to this book and whose heart and vision have stayed with me throughout its writing. As George Harrison once sang, "If not for you, Babe, I couldn't even find the door."

ONE

THE FLIGHT OF THE EAGLE AND CONDOR

Once I sat upon a promontory,
And heard a mermaid on a dolphin's back
Uttering such dulcet and harmonious breath,
That the rude sea grew civil at her song,
And certain stars shot madly from their spheres,
To hear the sea-maid's music.

WILLIAM SHAKESPEARE

The winding path that led to this book began when an Ashaninca shaman, working in the jungle outside of Pucallpa, Peru, first alerted me to the deep affinities between the ancient Homeric world and the surviving indigenous cultures of the Amazon.

As Juan Flores, Susana, and I sat together by a stream that cascaded from pool to pool beneath the forest canopy, Juan, whose appearance as a stoic *indio* belies his zany sense of humor and large repertoire of stories and songs, unfolded his vision of the underwater creatures of present-day Amazonian cosmology. "The *sirenas* [Spanish for *mermaid*]," he said, "send messages when they sing—their song is very sad and can move anyone. So when they want to enchant someone, they come forth and sing.

1

You can hear them, but it has to be in a moment of deep silence and you are left deeply moved."

At Juan's words, the Sirens of ancient Greek mythology, whose rapturous song nearly seduced Odysseus and his men into abandoning their homeward voyage, sprang to my mind. Few of us now, living at such a remove from exposure to the raw elements endured by our ancestors, can fathom the power and danger of that song. Even in plain sight of the transfixed mariners withering away among the bones and corpses on the shore, Odysseus would have leapt off his ship and gladly swum into the Sirens' embrace—had he not been lashed to the mast.

Intrigued by the obvious kinship to their Amazonian cousins, I related Homer's account. Flores, who had never heard of the *Odyssey* before, listened with interest, but when I commented that the sirenas in the Amazon seemed more benevolent in disposition, the shaman grimaced and shook his head. I then recalled that Juan had earlier related to us a tragic event in his family. His sister had been abducted while swimming in a river by a *yacuruna*, or merman, and has since been transformed into an underwater being—a Siren.

Most of us are familiar with the gods and heroes of the works of Homer. The divine figures of Zeus hurling thunderbolts; Poseidon stirring up the sea with his trident; Aphrodite, born of the sea spume, and her son, Eros, with his wounding arrows; Hermes, the messenger of the gods; and Athena, the goddess of heroic endeavor, still inhabit our imagination—just as the great heroes of the ancient world do: Achilles in his battle rage, wily Odysseus stowed inside his Trojan Horse, discreet Penelope holding off her suitors, Hercules in his labors, and Jason sailing with his Argonauts.

Yet we keep these ancient figures at a distance, like quaint, elderly relatives living in backwater towns whose way of life is no longer relevant. Most of us know the ancient Greek world now through dreary high school readings of Homer or fluffy Hollywood re-creations. Few, especially among the professional classicists of our major universities, would be caught praying to Hermes for guidance in a tight spot!

It came as a surprise, therefore, when during our time living in the Amazon I began to discover that there were not only deep parallels between

*Fig. 1.1. Juan Flores with an image of a yacuruna, a dolphin-man,
wearing a manta ray as a hat, an eel as a belt, and fish as shoes.
Above and to the right of the yacuruna, with her tail visible, hangs
a European mermaid, an image adopted by Amazonian people
under the influence of the Spanish.*

the cosmologies of the present-day Amazonian peoples and the ancient
Indo-European Greek and Celtic cultures, but also common ways of seeking knowledge and reckoning with issues of disease and healing. So strong
are these affinities that Odysseus can be seen as having fundamental character traits and attitudes in common with the shamans of the Amazon.

The origin of this book, then, began in 2004, when I tagged along with
my coauthor, Susana, to the Amazon to study the healing potential of the
plants used by the shamans in the rain forest.* Susana's research centered
on the therapeutic use of *icaros,* the "magical melodies" of the shamans.
She was particularly interested in their role in intense healing experiences
in ceremonies with a psychoactive plant known as ayahuasca. I wanted to
write a good travel narrative that explored, from the inside, the process of
healing with traditional plant medicines. But as Susana and I accustomed

---

*My work *The Jaguar That Roams the Mind* offers a narrative account of this yearlong
pilgrimage.

ourselves to living within a cosmology where streams hosted *mer*-folk, trees were sentient like Tolkien's ents, and shamans had a curious symbiotic relationship with jaguars, I eventually faced the anthropologist's dilemma: How much can a researcher, committed to experiencing the paradigm shift necessary to understand his subject from *within*, allow his grip on an "objective" worldview to loosen? Will he not risk, as he raises the shaman's potion to his lips, falling into naïveté, or even going native?

The Siren song of the Amazon, with its hauntingly beautiful cultures and wild creatures, its great waterways and star-dripping night skies, seemed to hold us captive. Beyond the daily struggle of adaptation in the rain forest sounded a great chant, a thing of inestimable beauty, which drew us, Circe-like, into its inner chamber. How could even the most rational among us, having heard that song of primordial Nature, turn a deaf ear?

As well, the more deeply we entered into the lifeway of our maestro, Juan Flores (appropriately enough, *Johnny Flowers* in English), the more the internal logic of his indigenous cosmos revealed itself to us. There was, in fact, a thread that led through the maze of the shaman's experience, but we had to deposit our cultural baggage at the door to walk it.

Even in the rough conditions of field research, I was able to observe one of the intriguing side effects of immersion in indigenous lifeways that still survive in the Amazon rain forest: a dawning sense of the inner worlds of ancient cultures, whose lives were rounded with similar experiences and interpretations.

Such understanding didn't arrive like a bolt of lightning, but accrued through moments of reflection when the odd parallels between my experience and those of the figures of ancient literature struck me, or when I stumbled onto a surprising explanation for a bit of ancient Greek or Celtic culture. At the time, I saw them as interesting insights or footnotes, and nothing more—a natural outcome of immersion in an indigenous culture. I also occasionally found comfort, I confess, in reflecting on long-suffering Odysseus's journey home!

After many moons had passed over the jungle's canopy, I began to reflect that such immersions in ancient lifeways are analogous to an archaeological dig into the underlying layers of human consciousness, as literal in their own way as archaeologist Heinrich Schlieman's excavations at Troy. Perhaps, I began to suspect, the cultural parallels between the ancient Europeans and contemporary Amazonian peoples were not coincidental, that in the words of archaeological researcher Paul Devereux, "Deep down in time and consciousness, there must have been an underlying shamanic impulse that led to these forms of expression."[1]

Upon our return to our home in the San Francisco Bay Area, I stepped to the front of a college classroom and chose, serendipitously, to teach the *Odyssey*. As I worked with my students, the pieces of the puzzle of that deep affinity began to fall into place. Much as the constellations of the night sky will leap forward once one has learned to discern their forms, the matrix of plant/spirit/animal relations in Homer revealed the indigenous origin of his epics.

This shouldn't be too surprising. After all, story survives as a fossilized remnant of human experience and, as do fossils of extinct species, when approached correctly can yield unique perspectives into the lifeways of human cultures of the past.

Even more intriguing, I began to discern the outlines of a fragment of myth, or mythologem, in the heart of the struggle between Odysseus and the blinded Cyclops. This struggle seemed to capture Western civilization's emerging violent rupture with its native self—and, within the symbolic language of oral literature, to presage dire consequences. In short, it appeared to have all the characteristics of a prophecy.

This idea that the *Odyssey* contained such a remnant perplexed me, and the larger significance of this recognition of the native roots of Western culture did not begin to come into focus until we began to participate in the peyote ceremonies of the Native American Church (NAC). As Susana and my engagement in the peyote way deepened, so did our awareness of the indigenous prophecy: When the Condor of the south flies with the Eagle of the north, a new day for Earth will awaken!

This prophecy,* popularly attributed to the pre-Conquest Incans

---

*Please see appendix B, "The Prophecy of the Eagle and Condor," for a more in-depth discussion of the origin and character of this prophecy.

and now widely accepted both among the Native and Euro-American communities, speaks of a time in ancient history when the human family chose to separate into two different family paths. One path, according to anthropologist Jeff Jenkins, is represented by the Condor, "the path of the feminine, ritual, spiritual, the heart and intuition, and the indigenous world." The other path, represented by the Eagle, is the path of "the masculine, the mind, the material world and its control, and the industrial world."[2]

The prophecy claims that, according to the ancient Incan calendar, the close of the twentieth century is the time when the deadly strife between the Eagle and Condor peoples is to draw to a conclusion. They now have the possibility to fly and mate together in a creative symbiosis to restore and regenerate the Earth community.

A marker of this sea change is the emerging unification of indigenous peoples and traditions, North and South, as well as the "indigenizing" of Westerners previously without a native consciousness of connection to the Earth and its larger, nonhuman community.

In this way, the Eagle of the North came to us in the form of Hopi prophecy, whose cosmology also speaks of an awakening of the indigenous mind in our time. For this ancient culture, such awakening is necessary to cross the bridge from the disintegrating trajectory of modern society back to the way of "one heart," the only safe route through our present age—the Great Purification. Of course, between the underground kivas of the Hopis or the astronomical temples of the Maya, where prophecy of world-shaking events was received in ancient times, and contemporary apocalyptic fantasies lies a vast distance. Yet somehow those indigenous visions have migrated through the time depths to ignite our contemporary imagination.

Perhaps this is because, like other beings of myth, prophecy roams from mind to mind. One of the farther-flung components of a culture's cosmovision (or what we call, from a safe distance, a mythological system), prophecy arises from a confluence of visions, dreams, trance states, and artistic inspiration. It is also, like a dream, curiously elusive to pin down—official, priestly versions may eventually be engraved on calendrical stones at the feet of pyramids and jungle astronomical observatories, but only after the prophecy has simmered among the people, in many local variations, for many seasons.

In addition, prophecy only becomes truly relevant when it's heard. Prophecy is not a fact. Rather, it is a thing received, taken to heart so it catalyzes change in a person's life. Like cosmovision, prophecy may lose its savor when written down. It becomes an official version, an object of critique, something true or false in a factual sense, or an object of veneration. Yet prophecy is not a fact—it is a living current, like the sap that flows through the veins of leaves. In constant evolution, there is no orthodox version. The stream continues to flow through Hopi kivas and other sacred sites.

I therefore never paid serious attention to all the buzz around 2012. After all, documents are always open to interpretation, facts shift their meaning according to methodology, and, like the children's game of telephone, transmission over distance is fraught with error. We have the Earth under our feet, its plants and animals and waters, and the stars above us to show us the way. What subtler prophecy could we be privy to?

Then one day, I heard the Hopi prophecy. It came one voice removed from its source, in the person of Bob Boyll, a seventy-five-year-old roadman, or "one who shows the path," in the NAC, who has lived many years among the indigenous communities of the United States and Mexico.

Fig. 1.2. Roadman Bob Boyll and his wife, Ann Rosencranz

I first met Boyll, whose ancestry is Scots-Irish and Mohawk, when I stepped through the flap of a tipi where a peyote meeting was about to begin. A stocky man with gray hair held back in a ponytail, he greeted me with an abstracted, kindly air. Thinking, "Ah, he's a cool old hippy," I went to take my seat. This was my first meeting, and that evening I had the privilege of beholding a sacred fire, which, it turned out, Boyll, in the role of fireman, was assisting the roadman in keeping.

At some point, as my visions and dreams danced in the fireplace, I became aware that the old man wading through the coals was working a kind of alchemy. Boyll's hands seemed to commune with the fire, to transmute it, like an ancient Celtic god of blacksmithery, into something magical. In the morning, when he talked about the various intelligences— beings, actually—perceivable within the flames of the fire, I realized that Boyll had, as they say, seriously done his homework.

As part of Boyll's long apprenticeship in the indigenous ways of medicine work, he had sought instruction from the Hopis who live in the village of Hotevilla on Arizona's First Mesa. The year was 1978, a time in his life when he was seeking answers to questions his graduate program in philosophy at Columbia had not addressed, among which were the visionary abilities of the Hopis.

Boyll relates that, arriving unannounced at one of the stone mortar houses of the village, he was greeted by a sharp-eyed woman in her nineties, who upon opening the door declared, "Oh, you're finally here! He's been waiting for you all morning!"

Astonished, Boyll was shown into the main room, where a hale and very old blind man sat, who embraced him, saying, "Oh, grandson, you're finally here!" The Hopi was named David Monongue, and his age was then estimated at 107. Monongue immediately inquired if Boyll had brought one of those recording machines, and being told yes, sent him back out to the car to retrieve it. Monongue had something to transmit, and wanted to make sure it got recorded accurately.

That afternoon the elder Hopi sang for Boyll the butterfly kachina song. "When you're in ceremony I want you to sing this," he explained, stating that he was giving it to Boyll because, as a song of unification, it contained all the colors of the rainbow. "The time has come," he said, "for a regathering of everyone, not just the Hopis, into unity." Boyll now sings it in sweat lodges he leads throughout the United States and Europe.

One afternoon during the week that Boyll spent with Monongue, the old man took him out to the Second Mesa, where one of the prophecy rocks of the Hopis, part of a sandstone cliff formation covered with ancient carvings, rises twenty feet high.*

Fig. 1.3. The Hopi prophecy stone

The main petroglyph shows a figure representing the Earth guardian, Maasau'u, who welcomed the original humans, who for the Hopis emerged from under the Earth and lived unified with them for many years under the covenant they made with him. In the hand of Maasau'u is a staff, from

---

*Boyll is careful to specify that, among the Hopi, prophecy is transmitted only in ceremonial context by reciters—individuals specially appointed and trained for the task. At the same time, for those of us who are not qualified to deliver prophecy, it is permissible to share it among friends and community. Boyll is, therefore, sharing the prophecy with us, not reciting it.

which emerges a square representing an original condition of wholeness. Eventually, however, discord arose and migrations away from the mesas took place.*

From this square, therefore, two lines set off across the face of the stone representing roads. On the upper line are human figures whose bodies progressively disintegrate, first with the loss of the solar plexus, and then with their heads drifting away from their bodies. These figures are known as the people of "two hearts," signifying a state of spiritual disunity, and their road grows progressively jagged and then breaks apart, indicating disintegration, chaos.

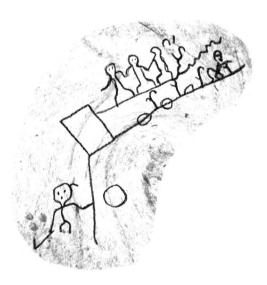

Fig. 1.4. Detail of the petroglyph on the Hopi prophecy stone

This disintegration is a period of geological upheaval and societal discord and collapse, but this emerging chaos is also called by the Hopis the "Great Purification," indicating its spiritual significance. According

---

*Among those who migrated were the ancestors of the European whites, who the Hopis say traveled until they came to a wall, on which they knocked their foreheads four times and then turned around and headed back. "I've seen that wall!" Monongue declared, "It's in Jerusalem," evidently referring to the Wailing Wall.

to Monongue, whatever is not essential to our being, anything that draws the heart away from unity, will be consumed, and there will be an opportunity to return to the lower road of the petroglyph, the way of "one heart." In fact, a "bridge" can be seen connecting the two roads, indicating a moment of opportunity that will occur in each individual's life when the passage opens to go from two-hearted to one-hearted, or vice versa. A second bridge exists as well, giving a certain leeway for those who wish to return. Once the second bridge is traversed, however, there is no departing from one's chosen road.

This lower road Monongue described as the way of those who know where they belong on Earth, and that they belong *to* the Earth. It is the way of those who have returned to their clans. The Hopi vision, it is worth noting, is the opposite of the Garden of Eden myth, which depicts our ancestors as cast out of the clan's original dwelling place to wander in exile, unable to return to the original connection to the Garden because an angel with a flaming sword stands guard at the entrance to the sacred land.

In the Hopi petroglyph, the road appears lined with stalks of corn and mounds, and the leader of the path of the one heart is there, the figure of a man holding a planting stick in his hand, planting corn. It is a humble, yet very inviting image.

If wisdom arises from such simple communion with the Earth, then the Hopis may be able to remind us of it. The planting stick held in this figure's hand was, and still is, used to plant corn in the desert, which makes it a stick for planting prayers,* for each seed, for the Hopis, is a prayer. One might smile and say, "It's good to pray if you're going to plant in such arid conditions."

The Hopis would most likely agree. So prayerful are they that they don't irrigate their corn. They summon the rain instead. Boyll witnessed the Hopis' intimate connection with their ecological system one day when he attended a dance to the kachina spirits who govern the rainfall.

---

*Perhaps in recognition of the intimate relationship between prayer and agriculture, each family's planting stick in Hopi culture is stored in the underground kivas when it's not in use.

"The sky went from arid, deep blue from one horizon to the next to pouring rain by the dance's conclusion," he reported. "The rain literally came out of the blue."

According to Monongue, one of the signs of the approach of the Great Purification—and there are many—would be the desire of people to reform their clans. To Boyll, he said, "You're still looking for your original home, but after all the migrations the time has come when your people can find where they belong." Monongue, whose language has no verb to express the concept "to be," meant something bigger than just physical locale. He meant belonging to the cosmos, which is expressed by a clan's spiritual communion with its ancestors, sacred topography, medicines, animal allies, songs, origin myths, dreams, and sacred art, even ways of growing food, treating water, or raising children—all those cultural practices that express a vital, living participation in a sentient world.

When Boyll asked Monongue, "Grandfather, how did you know I was going to appear at your doorstep on the day I did?" the old man explained to him that, for the Hopis, transmigration occurs not individually but in clans, much as birds migrate not solo but in flocks. These soul groups come in and out of existence, and are attracted to one another, consciously or not, each time they come back into incarnation.

"You are my grandson. We know this, and it cannot be changed," Monongue said. "In kiva ceremony I saw you were about to arrive."

Monongue also said that every sacred fire, kiva ceremony, or peyote meeting—that is to say, every time of collective transformation and evolution among the people—has an attendant spirit. This living being exists long before the event, containing and directing it, and is precognizant of what specific work needs to be done in each participating individual's life.

In a similar vein, these soul groups are preexisting clans, whose members, especially in the time of the Great Purification, are called to find one another. This spiritually directed regathering strongly suggests that the bridge between the roads of the two-hearted and one-hearted is the way from our collective identity with nation-states and corporations (and their suicidal tendencies) to individuated kinship within clans, clans who follow the leader of the path of one heart.

Monongue also expressed his belief in the need for renewal among the native peoples of the Americas, many of whom now live caught between two worlds. "It is late for us," he said. "Our cultures have become hardened into systems without connection to their source."

"Essentially, then," I asked Boyll, "Monongue was saying we need to go native again."

"Yes," Boyll responded. "That's it."

This is, according to Monongue's transmission to Boyll, the summons within the Hopi prophecy for us—to awaken the indigenous mind, to rediscover our clans as the path of one heart through the Great Purification. This summons in now in effect. Boyll states that we may even find ourselves strongly moving toward, or suddenly within, a state of constant prayer—a sign, as they say, of the times.

Such awakening may not be as distant from us as we think. It may be just around the corner, if we only look for it. As a Crow elder once told poet Gary Snyder, "You know, I think if people stay somewhere long enough— even white people—the spirits will begin to speak to them. It's the power of the spirits coming up from the land. The spirits and the old powers aren't lost, they just need people to be around long enough and the spirits will begin to influence them."[3]

Yet we must *listen,* and listen hard, not only to our native elders, but to the spirits of the land and our ancestors if we are to reawaken our native mind. A piece of that endeavor, I believe, is to hear the great, ancient songs anew, to open ourselves, after centuries of rationalist obscuration, to the glorious, strange, wild beauty of our native Western European inheritance.

Incan astronomers saw figures in the dark regions of the sky, as well as among the points of light. For them, the heavens were not a blank slate of darkness for a geometer's theories to overlie, but a dense, fecund canopy of spreading boughs and waterways—a populated ecosystem, a wild terrain. My favorite constellation, pointed out to Susana and me during a recent visit to Chile, was a serpent that wove itself through the foliage of the Milky Way. A couple of stars marked its gleaming eyes.

A similar elusiveness seems to characterize indigenous prophecy. If you can catch a clear glimpse of it in the foliage, you got lucky! If prophecy does weave itself into our existence, it does so chameleon-like, nestled into the dense forest of our lives so that we may never catch a glimpse of its emerald eyes regarding us from the canopy.*

Yet even as the ancestral voices of the Mayan, Incan, and Hopi cultures, arriving like exotics from over the horizon, give us unsettling evidence that Western society exists only as a brief chapter within a larger movement of humanity, we remain oddly deaf to the voices of the European ancestors, those great singers of the ancient world, who also participated in a living, sentient cosmos and were inheritors of a centuries-old oral tradition, deeply rooted in indigenous lifeways.

This work, then, is an attempt to gather the ancient European tradition back into the native fold, to approach the song of Homer anew and invoke the Muse to "sing for our time, too."†

---

*Only after I wrote this section did Boyll point out to me that David Monongue's name means "chameleon" in Hopi.

†The original Greek of this passage is *eipe kai hemin,* which simply means "speak to us." This is a direct invocation of the Muse, but one that clearly suggests the meaning Robert Fagles (whose translation I use throughout) gives it in his translation.

TWO

SNAKE MEDICINE

A snake which gets wounded heals itself. If now this is done by the snake, do not be astonished for you are the snake's son. Your father does it, and you inherit his capacity, and therefore you are also a doctor.

PARACELSUS

One of the most compelling litmus tests of the worth of any culture's cosmovision is this question: How is healing realized within it?

Such a query strikes to the heart of the unique value (and efficacy) of any culture's folklore, since the art of healing is among the most subtle of interactions with the living cosmos of the body and the natural, cultural, and spiritual worlds in which it flourishes.

That Homer's *Odyssey* is concerned with healing is suggested by its name in Greek: *Nostos* (Homecoming). This is especially true if the root of *nostos* "implies a return of consciousness (*noos*) in a 'coming back' from Hades."[1] That is, a return from the realm of the dead.

The *Odyssey*, in this sense, can be seen as an awakening song, a healing song, if it is understood at its deepest root. As the songs of the bards within the epic poem serve to restore consciousness and, as we shall see, heal, the song of Odysseus's struggle to return home can be understood in the same light. The greatest threat faced by Odysseus and his men on

15

their otherworld journey, after all, is not physical danger or death, but oblivion—loss of consciousness of home, being swallowed up in the waters of *Lēthē,* forgetting.

In this way the *Odyssey* betrays a deep affinity with the cosmovision of indigenous peoples, who similarly perceive disease as a consequence of unconsciousness, of being in disharmony with the cosmos they believe the diseased soul can be sung back into harmony again.

The Kuna peoples of Panama, for example, see sickness as a manifestation of a lack of attunement to the story of the cosmos and heal by singing the song of the Earth and universe back into the diseased member. Among the Tzutujil Maya:

> the world is a sacred building called the House of the World and our individual bodies are made like this House of the World and contain everything that exists in the outer world. The way the initiated shaman heals the person is to rebuild the World House of that person, remembering all its parts back to [the original flowering]. Welcoming all the parts back to life entails singing out a sacred map of ordered holy words and magical sounds. This is a microcosm of the macrocosmic Divine Order of the Original World Body. This sacred map re-creates all the sacred mountains, rivers, trees, springs, ancestral regions, and names of Gods and Goddesses and their abodes. When this song is sung properly, the individual song is harmonized with the Great Song of the Original World House and both the individual and the collective are made well again.[2]

It is appropriate, therefore, to begin with an example of how indigenous medicine can heal disease considered incurable by Western medical science, a feat that strongly suggests that the healing ways of the ancient Greeks and native peoples continue, even today, with unabated vitality.

Not so long ago, emerging from the Amazon rain forest, I found a message awaiting me to call home. Speaking from the other side of the Western Hemisphere, Susana asked me if our friend, the Ashanincan curandero

Juan Flores, whom I had been visiting at Mayantuyacu, his center for traditional medicine, could heal a rare case of snakebite. Turning to Juan, who was seated beside me in his noisy office in Pucallpa, I posed the question to him.

"Yes," he answered simply, with the traditional authority of a shaman to an apprentice. Without pausing to ask for specifics, I relayed his response and a chain of events was set in motion that demonstrated the remarkable efficacy of indigenous, shamanic medicine. It was not, in fact, a mere snakebite that Juan was called on to heal, but a severe case of chronic inflammatory demyelinating polyneuropathy, or CIDP (according to Western medicine, an incurable degenerative disease), which had occurred as a consequence of severe rattlesnake envenomation.

Upon returning to the United States, I was introduced to Nick, the man seeking treatment with Juan. I recognized him as someone I had seen around the tipi meetings of the Native American Church. Laconic, dressed in black, and constantly smoking, Nick walked in heavy boots with a Boris Karloff gait that I had found puzzling. Whenever he spoke in meetings, his words commanded respect, and it was clear that his participation in the peyote way of the Plains Indians was longstanding.

Nick, it turned out, had been bitten by a rattlesnake at its height of venomousness, and years later he was suffering severely degenerative effects from the toxins. He lived with pain—constant, intense burning in his lower legs, which extended up to his hips; painful cramping in his feet and hands; constant twitching (fasciculation) throughout his limbs; nightly cold sweats; loss of motor control; and an "indescribable" feeling of electric current in his extremities. Heavy orthopedic boots encased his numbed feet.

His long ordeal to find a cure had even led him to contemplate a radical, very dangerous experimental treatment that would have knocked his immune system "into the Dark Ages" through chemotherapy, but in the end Western technological medicine simply had no solutions for him. In the process of embracing his disease as an initiatory path, rather than a mere stroke of terrible misfortune, Nick had been astonished to find his own medicine of the desert chaparral, peyote, sending him on a quest for a cure in the Amazon with the rainforest medicine ayahuasca.

Indigenous medicine comes wrapped in paradox for Westerners. Among these paradoxes is the distinction between curing and healing of disease, concepts that, as in Venn diagrams, overlap yet remain experientially distinct. The general thrust of modern, industrial Western medicine is to "cure," from Latin *cura*, "to care, concern, trouble," by either suppressing symptoms (that is, managing disease) or excising it from the body. Treatment is considered satisfactory when symptoms abate or lessen so that the life of the sufferer is more tolerable. In many indigenous styles of medicine, which give equal importance to curing as the West, healing, from Old English *haelan*, "to make whole, sound and well," may also involve searching out the hidden origin of the disease in the body-mind. In other words, there is a teaching contained within disease that must be heard, understood, and heeded. The patient must, in short, *remember* her or his way back to health, to harmony with the cosmos.

In this healing quest, a cure may be found or it may not. The valence of the disease, however, will change. In such cases, it is the entire self that is engaged in unraveling a disease's enigma, and the entire organism is the laboratory wherein the cure and/or healing can be found. As a consequence, such healing is always idiosyncratic, because each body's laboratory is unique.

For Western medicine, if disease is cured shamanically, the methodology used (which in *vegetalismo* is a complex synergy of plants, the shaman's icaros—or sacred songs—and the ecology of the healing locale itself) will often elude scientific researchers in search of a "silver bullet" molecule. The medicine may be frustratingly nonexportable—its efficacy may vanish as soon as it is separated from the culture that gave rise to the healing in the first place.*

In our experience, the plant medicines used in the Amazon, among which the visionary plant ayahuasca is only one, do healing work, but may

---

*See chapter 7 of my *Jaguar That Roams the Mind*, as well as chapter 6 in this book, for discussions of healing/cures of brain tumors through indigenous methods that elude Western methodologies.

not always bring about a cure. Whether it is worthwhile to cure a disease without healing the conditions that gave rise to it is not something that Western medicine considers very much, but if a disease is bringing an urgent life message to the patient, it may be folly to suppress its teaching. This, of course, is a paradox for many Westerners, who prefer, as poet Robert Bly once put it, the freedom to stagger from Burger King to Burger King over taking full responsibility for their spiritual, psychological, and physical conditions.[3]

Nick had already experienced healing in indigenous ways. As he told us, at age twenty-nine, while undergoing alcohol withdrawal, he had suffered a cardiac infarction that scarred his heart. After his heart attack, he developed an arrhythmia, a violent limp of the heart that was deeply unsettling: "My heart would beat *one . . . two . . . da dung*. It would then stop and pick up again. It was so loud you could hear it."

A friend suggested that Nick seek healing in the NAC, since Western medicine had basically written him off as not long for this world. Nick had deep apprehensions, however: "As an addict, for me a medicine like peyote could be construed as a drug, and I had real concerns about risking my sobriety."

Peyote, however, has a venerable history of usage to heal alcoholism and other sicknesses. A cactus with psychoactive properties, peyote has been used in ceremonial contexts for thousands of years by the native peoples of the Americas, both as a medicine to align the spirit with the cosmos and to heal the body of disease. Overcoming his trepidations, Nick chose to attend a meeting.

The roadman for the meeting was Bob Boyll, who after Nick explained his heart condition, told him, "Well, there's no reason you can't be healed, but it is not going to be me healing you. It's really contingent on whether you've learned the lesson that you needed to learn by having your heart be that way."

Something in Boyll's words resonated with Nick. As Nick put it, "I was like: *huh*." Right around midnight, Boyll went and fed Nick four medicine balls of peyote. Nick, bewildered, tried to focus on what was happening around him as Boyll fanned him with an eagle fan. "Then he took the eagle bone whistle and blew it right into my heart and I felt the arrhythmia leave. It wasn't just me who saw it, either." At that same instant the fire, which was stacked up blazing about three feet high, dramatically flattened all the way down to the ground as if some unseen foot had stomped on it.

"The heart condition was gone. Forever. Just like that." Nick laughed. "That's kind of what got me coming around the NAC, you know? I felt obligated, like I owed my life to whatever it was that saved me."

Boyll gives an intriguing advisory to those who seek healing on the medicine path: "Once you begin walking this sacred way, the stakes get raised and you get scheduled for a series of initiations. Your entire life becomes a test." It is another paradox of indigenous medicine: life becomes more challenging and obstacle-filled after healing than before.

A couple of years later, Nick and his partner, Lisa, made a journey to Loch Loman Reservoir in Santa Cruz. It was a morning marked by strange omens. On the way, a fleeting illness struck them both at the same moment, numbing their faces and cramping their insides; it then vanished as quickly as it had come.

Then, at the lake, an enigmatic exchange occurred. A golden eagle flew across the sky and Nick called out to it, "Please drop a feather for me. Please drop a feather." As soon as the eagle flew above them, it dropped a feather. Straight down. Nick hastily clambered into a rowboat and started out on the water to fetch it, but someone in an electric boat zoomed out of nowhere, picked up the feather, and stuck it in his hat. Nick, affronted, called out, "Hey, man, I asked for that feather. I asked that bird for that feather and it's mine." The man in boat shrugged, said, "Too bad you don't have an electric rowboat," and took off.

"Ten minutes later, the snake bit me," Nick concluded.

It was only in Peru, while working with ayahuasca and jergon sacha, the traditional antidote for snakebite, prescribed by Flores, that Nick received a revelation of what had actually transpired that day. "I asked that bird for what I wanted," Nick said, "but it directed me to what I needed. The eagle is a high-energy creature, of the astral. The serpent is the energy of the Earth. At that point in my life I was freshly sober, like a little kid. My priorities were all out of whack. That feather belonged to that guy who got it. What happened to me was I got directed to that snake, because that's what I needed in my life—even though I didn't want it, even though it's taken a huge chunk of my life. That medicine down in Peru showed me the truth of the matter."

On that fateful day in Santa Cruz, like a naïve Persephone, Nick plucked a narcissus flower that abducted him into Hades. "I've always fancied myself the amateur herpetologist. I've owned snakes my whole life. I've raised pythons, poisonous snakes. I see this rattlesnake sitting there, maybe ten years old, with black and white stripes. The kind they call coontails. I said to Lisa, 'Should I catch it?' She said, 'Nah. Leave it alone.' She already knew I knew how to handle reptiles, but my pride got the better of me and I reached out to grab it." Just at that moment the snake shifted position and was able to swing around and get its fangs in his finger. Pulling it off, still holding it in his hand, Nick grimly announced to Lisa, "Uh, I just got bit."

Sometimes snakes will dry-bite, but Nick knew immediately that he'd been envenomated. "My hand was on fire. I felt like I weighed a million pounds." To add insult to injury, the rattlesnake was close to hibernation, a time when a snake's venom is most poisonous, containing both neurotoxins and hemotoxins, which attack nerve cells, burst capillaries, and destroy tissue and blood. As a result, the snake injected a more lingering poison into him than the reptile would have in another season.

Lisa managed to transport Nick back across the lake to the ranger station, where a helicopter was immediately called. On his way to the hospital, Nick felt his heart racing out of control as the venom liquefied his blood. "You know what?" he said to himself, "this feels like I could die." Then a voice said, "Don't worry, you're going to be fine." At that moment, looking up, he could see his heart rate immediately slow on the monitor, and heard the paramedic reassure him, "Ah, that's good, you're going to make it."

At the hospital, Nick's hand still felt like it was stuck in fire. "Not only was my whole body shaking and quivering, like there were bees flying around under my skin, but I looked like I was the Michelin tire guy. They were sticking needles in my arm to check the pressure because they thought they might have to lance it. Fortunately, it never got that bad, but they did give me enough antivenom medicine for four people and four platelet transfusions." Finally, the toxicity of the venom began to wane, but Nick's system had been left devastated.

"Most people bitten by rattlesnakes are there for a day—three tops. I was there for fifteen days. Not only that, when I got out I went back to the doctor and after doing a blood test they said, 'Holy shit, you have no platelets! Don't bump into anything!' and I went back to the hospital for another four days. If I'd bumped into something, I could have hemorrhaged and bled to death."

In the *Santa Cruz Sentinel,* the headline read, "Man, 31, Bitten by Snake Trying to Impress Girlfriend."

"You know," Nick concluded, "ego is the number-one killer of men."

The doctors eventually gave Nick a clean bill of health, and he thought he'd left this episode of his life behind him.

Then, a couple of years later, Nick was playing music and the fingers of his right hand stopped working. "'Move,' I said to them, but they wouldn't move." Within days this paralysis progressed, allowing him to squeeze but not extend his hand. Nick began to make the rounds of the local hospitals. "I get all these tests, visit three different neurologists, and I finally end up with one of the best-known doctors in Santa Cruz, who said he thought I had Lou Gehrig's disease." Nick knew what that was—"It's a death sentence. Ninety percent of the people who get it die within three years of diagnosis." Nick lived with that diagnosis for almost a year, but then he began to notice that it wasn't progressing the way he'd read about it. As he described his diagnosis of multifocal motorneuropathy, a form of the autoimmune disease called chronic inflammatory demyelinating polyneuropathy, to me, I commented, "You learned a lot of heavy terminology during this time."

"Well, I'll tell you," he said, "there's a positive and negative to everything. The negative side to learning Western medicine is you get sucked in. If you suffer from an ailment, you get sucked into the doctor's way of thinking about it, which is God-cold and no resolution."

"God-cold?" I asked.

"Yeah, Western medicine has no God in it, and there's no resolution for CIDP. They call it an incurable chronic disorder. They have medicines that can slow it down, but no cure. I spent over a million dollars for an ineffectual Band-Aid.

"During the course of all this," he continued, "I tried to be as hopeful as possible, but finally I shut down and went into a black depression. I was brainwashed—by my own intellect and what doctors had told me—into accepting a hopeless diagnosis. I had given up and didn't care if I died the next day."

Finally, Lisa, now Nick's wife, called for a medicine sweat for their family. For Nick, it turned into a kind of intervention. Nick ate "a ton" of medicine, but could not relinquish his argumentative, self-righteous mind-set. Finally, Boyll, who was running the sweat, said to him, "I love you, but you know what? We're tired. We're tired of how you're being."

Nick finally confessed, "You know what? I don't know what to do."

Boyll replied, "Nick, you've been here before. You remember when you were here last time?"

Then Nick put it together. "I was right at the same place where I'd been with my booze. Where I gave up all hope and there was no place to go. I hit bottom right in the middle of a medicine sweat. I experienced all kinds of revelations, was able to see with clarity what I'd been doing, how my behavior had affected my family. My life changed, and I picked up the fight again, but in a different way. I recognized that there was a definite reason why I was going through what I was. It wasn't just a bunch of random circumstances. There was a plan to it."

Nick still didn't know what to do, but his confidence was growing again. He said to himself, "I'll leave it up to Creator and something will come along." A few weeks later, something did indeed come along.

In the dry hills of Tuolumne County, as a tipi was being set up for an NAC meeting, a rattlesnake was discovered sitting beneath a tarp in the exact location where the chief, or roadman, sits for a ceremony. Nick was present and watched as the snake was taken outside and set beneath a bush. Knowing he was at fault for messing with that species of snake a few years earlier, he took the opportunity to make amends. "I gave it some tobacco and prayed for forgiveness for putting myself in a position to harm it and myself."

That night, as he was sitting in the tipi, out of the clear blue sky the word *ayahuasca* came into his mind. "The peyote medicine was saying, 'You need to go and work with this medicine,'" Nick realized.

"I had heard of ayahuasca," he said, "but I'd never had any desire to try it—at all. *That's odd*, I thought. I doubted it immediately."

That evening, Nick said to Lisa, "You know, I just got this over-whelming message about working with ayahuasca. What is that?" Lisa had no idea. Nick wandered into the living room and, turning on the television, was greeted by the word *ayahuasca* emblazoned across the screen. It was a National Geographic program on Santo Daime.

That clinched it for Nick. "When people tell me stories like this, I don't normally believe them. With this one, though, I thought there's got to be something to this." Through Boyll and his partner, Ann Rosencranz, Nick got in contact with Susana and I.

Like peyote, ayahuasca has an ancient lineage in its own habitat, the Amazon rain forest. Its name arises from the joining of two words in Quechua: *aya,* which signifies "soul," "ancestor," or "spirit," and *huasca,* meaning "vine" or "rope." Ayahuasca, therefore, is the vine of the souls. Actually an admixture of the vine ayahuasca and (in Peru) the leaves of the chacruna tree, like peyote the ayahuasca brew is psychoactive, and evidence suggests it has been used for similar shamanic purposes for millennia.

Shamans in the vegetalista tradition who use this medicine, among whom Juan Flores numbers, are called ayahuasqueros, and consider it the master teacher among the many plants used within the native pharmaco-poeia. In Nick's case, ayahuasca was ancillary to his main treatment—the plant jergon sacha.

Upon arriving at Mayantuyacu, after many hours of air, land, and sea travel, Nick was immediately set at ease by the way Flores and his people began treating him as a patient, assuring him, "We're going to

Fig. 2.1. Juan Flores preparing ayahuasca

Fig. 2.2. Juan Flores with the jergon sacha plant at Mayantuyacu

get the venom out of you." He was also introduced to the jergon sacha plant, a powerful snake venom antidote from the native pharmacopoeia. Most likely originally identified by its "signature"—the mottling on its bark that closely resembles the patterning on the back of the venomous pit viper known as the jergon—the large bulb, or "stool," at the base of the plant has been used for generations to prevent and treat snakebite. Natives have long taken plant baths and rubbed themselves down with jergon sacha to protect themselves upon entering the jungle; sought it out and quickly applied it, with great efficacy, after snakebite; and used it to treat the lingering consequences of envenomation.

Flores told Nick that his problem was he was toxified—the venom was still in his body and needed to be released. Western doctors had told Nick the same thing. The enzymes of rattlesnake venom are magnetized by fat and go to the places in the body with the highest concentration of fat—the myelin sheath that covers nerves. As a result, Juan and a visiting doctor from Lima, who has been using jergon sacha to treat HIV,* explained that Nick's autoimmune system was attacking itself. Without removing the toxins that were at the source of the malfunctioning of his autoimmune system, no recuperation was possible. Nick already knew this as well—Western science had no way to remove the toxins from his body, so he had been taking immunosuppressants instead to reduce the symptoms. Juan was, in effect, informing Nick that the vegetalista tradition could do a lot better than that: it could actually cleanse his system of the venom.

Deeply encouraged, Nick began his *dieta,* the simple and direct method of Amazonian medicine where a patient drinks plant remedies that have been prepared by a curandero. Both the medicines and the patient are sung over with icaros, the magical melodies that contain and transmit the healing virtue of the plants. As well, ayahuasca ceremonies are used to better enable the curandero to direct the spirits of the plants and other "doctors," and for the patient to more thoroughly integrate the healing received.

---

*A handful of Peruvian doctors report using the antiviral properties of *jergon sacha* to treat HIV with great success, although there have yet to be any published clinical trials on the efficacy of this treatment.

Fig. 2.3. The "signature" on a jergon sacha plant, whose bark has markings resembling that of the jergon snake, thus indicating serpent medicine (Photo courtesy of Josh Nepon)

Jergon sacha had an immediate healing effect. In keeping with the plant's purgative power, upon drinking the preparation made by boiling its stool in water, Nick got quite ill: "It felt like I'd gotten bit by that snake again. I felt that same really heavy, heavy feeling, sweating, just sick as a dog. But they had said that might happen. I was drinking two liters of the plant medicine a day and the toxin was breaking up in my fatty cells and being rereleased into my bloodstream." After the initial nausea passed, however, Nick found he was recuperating rapidly. In short order the burning sensation and spasmodic jumping in his legs, which had kept him awake all night for years, vanished.

While jergon sacha is very effective as an antivenom, Flores explained to Nick that it was not going to be a quick fix because he had already sustained long-term damage, even skirted nerve death. Nick was therefore also given *came renaco,* a strangler vine of the Amazon rain forest whose muscular growth has led to its use to rebuild torn and degenerated muscle, ligaments, nerves, and bones. The combination of the two plants has been quite effective. Nerve conduction is returning to Nick's feet: one foot is entirely restored, and the other, which had degenerated so far that it felt as if "there was nothing there," is now partially alive again. Nick is hopeful that he can entirely rehabilitate. Recently, he sent out an image on Facebook of his discarded orthopedic boots.

Much as the rattlesnake had made an appearance at the tipi meeting where Nick was directed toward the medicine of the rain forest, the appearance of two venomous pit viper serpents heralded the successful conclusion of his treatment. On his last day at Mayantuyacu, within a single hour, a huge bushmaster—the most poisonous snake in the Western Hemisphere— came racing down the slope toward the little village. Then an equally impressive jergon, the serpent that bestowed its name on Nick's medicine, was discovered while clearing brush. Both were killed in the ensuing melee and their bodies brought and laid before an astonished Nick.

Nick's totemic snakes suggest that his journey was an initiatory one. As he told us, having experienced the chthonic powers of the serpent, it has "opened up doors where I know I can help people. The most powerful messages you can bring people have to come from a place of experience. My work helping alcoholics and addicts, and now handicapped people, was completely revolutionized. I don't just have a theoretical understanding of what it means to return from the dead. I've lived it."

One morning after an ayahuasca ceremony at Mayantuyacu, an Argentine healer approached Nick and told him, "Last night I saw this Native American old man sitting next to you and he was talking to me. He was saying that with everything you're going through, you're reaching a place in yourself where you can help and heal people."

"You know what else he told me?" Nick asked me. "He said, 'You know, the best healers are the wounded ones.'"

What Nick's rain forest quest indicates is that, unlike in Western technological medicine, Amazonian medicines are allies in a battle of the soul. In a similar way, Nick's recovery from an "incurable" disease can be seen as an initiatory path, one more akin to the Native American vision quest or a Buddhist monk withdrawing into the forest to practice meditation than a patient checking into a modern hospital to undergo treatment.

Far from being surpassed and rendered obsolete by our contemporary technological approaches, traditional medicine continues to flourish and reminds us of how profound healing can be when it arises from indigenous perception of a sentient, living cosmos.

THREE

POSEIDON'S CURSE

The Rupture with the Indigenous Mind

The powers, delaying, not forgetting, have
Incensed the seas and shores, yea, all the creatures,
Against your peace . . . and do pronounce by me
Ling'ring perdition, worse than any death
Can be at once, shall step by step attend
You and your ways; whose wraths to guard you from—
Which here in this most desolate isle else falls
Upon your heads—is nothing but heart's sorrow
And a clear life ensuing.

ARIEL, IN WILLIAM SHAKESPEARE'S
THE TEMPEST

If God is mythopoeic, man must become mythopathic.

J. R. R. TOLKIEN

Indigenous perception, as a Crow elder once suggested to poet Gary Snyder, may not only be poised to reassert itself if we just hunker down to the Earth again, but it may also be a natural mode of perception for human beings. Certainly the experience of a vital, aware cosmos is instinctual to children.

A friend of mine, Brian, related to me how, as a boy growing up in a rural area of Illinois, a raven used to come to him in his dreams. It taught him the kinds of things ravens know, and with Brian on its back, would take him flying over the landscape surrounding his home, showing him hidden things in the forest.

One night the raven took him to visit an old broken-down carriage from the previous century, decaying silently in an unvisited part of the woods. Upon waking, Brian bound out of bed and raced out to locate it, following the raven's instructions. It was there, sure enough, right where the raven had shown him.

For my friend, the visitations of the raven were a special gift, a source of love and companionship his family couldn't give him. "I actually looked forward to dreaming more than I did waking," he laughed. "That raven was my best friend." Brian needed kinship with the animal world to survive: his father abandoned him and his brother on the streets a few years later.

Brian's bond with the raven was broken, just as such magical perception has been educated and persecuted out of children and whole populations for centuries now, when he made the mistake of revealing the wealth of his inner world to his family. They scoffed. They ridiculed him. They called his sanity into question. With the seed of rational doubt and shame planted in his mind, the raven faded away.

Yet there is plenty of evidence that, even as adults, we can recuperate from the suppression of our native perception. We may even make these crossings into the indigenous mind and not fully recognize their implications.

As a young man, I had the opportunity to join a Zen Buddhist retreat in the wilderness of Death Valley in California. It was rigorous. We got up and began meditating well before dawn in the freezing cold and practiced silent mindfulness throughout the day's blazing heat as we walked, ate, and worked together. At night we sat in meditation again for a couple of hours beneath the stars, finally crawling into our sleeping bags in the shivery cold again, sometimes with light snowfall dancing in the beams of our flashlights.

After many days of practice, my perception started to loosen, to shift from the habitual, and I became susceptible to teaching from the ancient land. The moment came one evening as a primitive stone tool, found on the desert floor, made its round from hand to hand.

When it came to me I held it, and, feeling how it nestled familiarly in my palm, it was as if the hand that had once carefully fashioned it on the shore of a lake vanished long ago in geological time reached over the centuries to touch me.

With a sudden physical vertigo, I saw and felt the constellations in the sky of my mind wheeling backward, beyond 1492 into the time depths of *this* continent.

Wrenched free of the artificial, vision-constricting European time line that had been forced on my native perception of the world, I understood that my country, the United States of America, which my school textbooks had hammered into me was the most significant thing to ever happen to the Western Hemisphere, was a flash in the pan compared to the ancient cultures that inhabit it as their own.

Looking back, I suspect on that day I became the first among my English and Danish ancestors to set foot in the sacred topography of the New World, even to comprehend the lineage of the native peoples of the Americas. That intuition would ripen until it led me into the Amazon rain forest and compelled me to write this book.

Could it be that this sort of epiphany marks passage into indigenous myth time? To going native again? The founder of the Buddhist community I was practicing with was, in fact, Gary Snyder, who also wrote, "For the non–Native American to become at home on this continent, he or she must be born again in this hemisphere, on this continent, properly called Turtle Island."[1]

One of the characteristics of native perception is a symbiosis, or overlapping, of human consciousness with the consciousness of plants, animals, landscapes, and the other beings of the cosmos.*[2] Among some natives of New Caledonia, in the South Pacific, for example, the same words are used to name the parts of the human body and those of the plants and other species of their habitat. The skin of the body and the bark of trees share the same word, as do the flesh of human limbs and the pulp of fruits.† Unlike the concept of *participation mystique,* which denotes a confusion of human and nonhuman based in a primitive inability to distinguish subject from object, for native peoples the permeability of human consciousness with the other orders of creation is taken as a simple, empirical reality, one to be grateful for, for it constitutes the sacred dimension of our lives.

As Vernon Masayesva, a former Hopi tribal chairman and environmental activist, explains it:

> The Hopis say when you die, when every living thing dies, they join the cloud people. We rise from our grave as mist and we travel with them up to mountains. We come down as rain or snow. Then we take our long journey back home: the ocean, the underground aquifers. We're going home. We go home. We rest. We come back again. Western science has this same version, except the "we" is

---

*Indeed, even for modern perception, as M. Merleau-Ponty shows in his *Phenomenology of Perception,* there is no hard-and-fast division between an internal self and an external world. We are in constant symbiosis, overlapping with all phenomena, so that no line of demarcation can be clearly identified dividing self and other. As Merleau-Ponty describes it, "In so far as my hand knows hardness and softness, and my gaze knows the moon's light, it is as a certain way of linking up with the phenomenon and communicating with it. Hardness and softness, roughness and smoothness, moonlight and sunlight, present themselves in our recollection not pre-eminently as sensory contents but as certain kinds of symbioses, certain ways the outside has of invading us and certain ways we have of meeting this invasion."

†Unfortunately, such deep symbiosis with the ecosystem is often treated as an earlier, primitive stage of mental development. Medical historian Dr. González-Crussi, for example, comments that, "In this society, the body is not thought of as an independent entity but is indistinguishable from its surroundings" (*A Short History of Medicine,* 4). *Inseparable,* rather than *indistinguishable,* may be more accurate.

disconnected, totally, from the phenomenon, the cycle. We have no part in it. In our world view, we are the clouds, we are the rain that comes down.[3]

Among Amazonian cultures, native or of the mixed-race vegetalistas, such intimacy with the environment is a feature of ordinary life. As anthropologist Luis Eduardo Luna wrote, "In the general animistic Amazonian religious background of the various Indian tribes that existed, and still exist, in the Amazonian territories. . . . Nature is animated by spiritual powers which assume theoriomorphic and anthropomorphic nature when communicating with human beings."[4] As we discovered during our apprenticeship in the jungle, a tree such as the *pinshacayo* is seen both as a literal plant with healing properties for the bones and blood *and* as a doctoring spirit with a human form. As well, it has a symbiotic relationship with the *pinsha,* or toucan, which serves as its animal manifestation (for example, when you've drunk the bark of the tree over time, the cry of the toucan informs you that someone is approaching from a distance). Similarly, among the Koyukan in the northern forests in Alaska, the raven is not just a bird, reports anthropologist Richard Nelson, but "is many other things first, its form and existence as a bird almost the least significant of its qualities. It is a person and a power, God in a clown's suit, incarnation of a once-omnipotent spirit. The raven sees, hears, understands, reveals . . . determines."[5]

This symbiosis of plant, animal, human, and spiritual consciousness is woven through the narrative of the *Odyssey,* yet so subtly that the reader, and a scholar without sensitivity to indigenous ways of knowing, can easily pass it by all unawares. A lovely example occurs when Odysseus, having made shore after surviving a shipwreck by Poseidon, must find shelter from men and wild beasts to sleep.

In a grove not far from shore, he finds two entwined olive trees, "sprung from the same root, one olive wild, the other well-bred stock. No sodden gusty winds could ever pierce them, nor could the sun's sharp rays invade their depths, nor could a downpour drench them through and through, so dense they grew together" (*Odyssey* 5.527–32). The "gentle olive tree" is sacred to Athena, but not the "wild olive of Olympia," whose uncultivated condition the German philologist and scholar of Greek religion Walter Burkert associates with the realm of Poseidon.[6] Beneath this frontier marker between the wild and the civilized, between the realm of Poseidon and Athena, Odysseus can bed down safe from wild beasts and allow Athena to shower sleep on his eyes.

It is no accident the same species of tree, the olive, resides as the central column of Odysseus's bedroom in his ancestral home in Ithaca, constituting the immovable frame of his bed. As Odysseus relates, "There was a branching olive tree inside our court, grown to its full prime, the bole like a column, thickset. Around it I built my bedroom, finished off the walls with good tight stonework, roofed it solidly. . . . I shaped it plumb to the line to make my bedpost, bored the holes it needed with an auger, working from there I built my bed, from start to finish" (*Odyssey* 23.214–17, 23.222–24). Since Odysseus deliberately established the olive tree as the guardian of his sleep and the foundation of his marriage bed, it is no surprise that upon first escaping the wild ocean haunts of Poseidon to the cultivated, humane land of the Phaeacians, he finds refuge in its sheltering embrace, which is simultaneously the embrace of his spirit ally, Athena. The goddess of war, strategy, and heroic endeavor protects his sleep, sends visionary dreams, and even gives him counsel, mediated by her botanical manifestation. True to form, when Odysseus and Athena finally shed their disguises and meet face-to-face upon his arrival home on Ithaca, they promptly go and sit "by the sacred olive's trunk to plot the death of the high and mighty suitors" (*Odyssey* 13.426–27).

The *Odyssey* teaches us the same basic lesson as Nelson learned among the indigenous Koyukan, that "reality is not the world as it is perceived directly by the senses; reality is the world as it is perceived by the *mind* through the medium of the senses. Thus, reality in nature is not just what we see, but what we have *learned* to see."[7]

Nelson relates that, during the passing of an honored Koyukan elder, an old woman was moved to walk to the nearby shore of a lake, where:

she stood at the water's edge and sang Koyukan "spring songs" to a pair of loons that had been in the lake for several weeks. Shortly, the loons swam toward her until they rested in the water some fifty yards away, and there they answered her, filling the air with eerie and wonderful voices. When I spoke with her later, she said that loons will often answer spring songs this way. For several days people talked of how beautiful the exchange of songs had been that morning.[8]

Based on an analysis of the structure of bird languages, such interspecies communication is unlikely to happen, according to naturalist Maryjo Koch: "A bird is rarely fooled by a human's imitation of its call. Bird songs are so complex that an impersonator rarely even comes close. With some songs of 80 notes per second and up to 4 overlapping notes produced at once, it would take the entire Mormon Tabernacle Choir to give a proper approximation."[9] Could it be that it is the *mind* through which indigenous people engage the natural world that allows for such intimate connection?

Such intimacy is key to indigenous healing traditions. One researcher, Dr. Rosa Giove, witnessed a powerful demonstration of its efficacy in the case of a year-old baby into whose eye's lacrimal duct a larva had intruded itself, lodging between the ball and the socket. Such parasitic invasions of the body are not uncommon in the jungle, and Western medicine normally extracts them surgically with a scalpel. Giove observed with great interest, therefore, when the mother commenced to sing a peculiar little melody of clicking sounds over her baby's eye. Before long, the larva stirred and crawled out of the eye socket of its own volition. Deeply moved, Giove inquired how she had performed that remarkable feat, and the woman told her that she had sung in the language of the insect, imitating a mother's call to a baby of that particular species.[10] Such magical songs, which play important healing roles in both indigenous and ancient cultures, clearly have an unrecognized empirical basis.*

---

*Such wise women also flourished in preindustrial European peasant culture. As Storchenko relates in Gogol's "Ivar Fyodorovich Shponka and His Aunt," from *The Overcoat and Other Tales of Good and Evil,* "I've been in the habit of stopping my ears for the

One of the obstacles to perceiving the indigenous cosmos that underlies the *Odyssey,* as well as understanding the nature of indigenous perception, has been the mythological approach, which attempts to systematically objectify the experience of vital, living cosmovisions, most often overlooking the fact that in so doing, it subtly fossilizes cosmology. In other words, mythology is what cosmology looks like from the outside, from the remove of time or culture. The good news is, just as with fossils, where with the right approach we can get a glimpse of the living dinosaur, it is possible to reconstruct something of the vital cosmovisions of other past cultures. The bad news should be obvious—just take a look at the dinosaurs in the museums.

An episode from the life of mythologist Joseph Campbell gives an illustration of this paradox. Campbell was invited to witness a traditional ceremony among the Navajos, where he watched a shaman sit down beneath a parched desert sky in the midst of a severe drought and, with the support of his community, begin a rain chant.

Campbell, a well-educated individual from a nonindigenous background, looked on with amusement—the immutable physical laws of the universe were not going to alter their course because of a mere song! Then dark clouds began to form on the horizon. By the time the thunderclouds broke directly over their heads and the rain came pouring down, a delighted Campbell realized he had encountered something his own culture and scientific background were utterly incapable of accounting for.[11]

Yet for the Navajos, nothing inexplicable had occurred. With their tribal knowledge based on hundreds or thousands of years of culture, ceremony, medicine, and understanding of the natural world, they were simply living out their cosmology.

Another fundamental misapprehension is that "myths" are designed to bring about psychological transformation.

---

night ever since that damned incident in a Russian inn where a cockroach crawled into my left ear. I can't tell you what I've been through! My ear kept tickling and tickling—it nearly drove me mad! I was cured by one of our own peasant women. A simple old peasant woman, sir. And what do you think she did? Why, just whispered some incantations over me! What can you say about our doctors after that, sir? Some of these peasant women know a damn sight more than all these doctors!"

Because it imparts sacred knowledge, [myth] is always recounted in a ritualized setting that sets it apart from ordinary, profane experience, and can be understood in the solemn context of spiritual and psychological transformation. Mythology is the discourse we need in extremity. We have to be prepared to allow a myth to change us forever. Together with the rituals that break down the barrier between the listener and the story, and which help to make it his own, a mythical narrative is designed to push us beyond the safe certainties of the familiar world into the unknown.[12]

While no doubt true in certain circumstances, one of the characteristics of indigenous perception is that there is no hard-and-fast division between sacred and profane experience. That dichotomy is an invention of modern societies. As well, while it is learned, or absorbed through culture, the traditional knowledge of indigenous cultures is not designed to push us beyond our comfort zone. In fact, one would have to search long and hard to find an inner self awaiting revelation from above, in the classic Platonic or Augustinian fashion. Rather, traditional knowledge teaches us how to *see;* that is, how to interact responsibly and maturely with a living cosmos. It is concerned not so much with transformation as with harmony and equilibrium.*

At its worst, the stratifications devised by mythologists in the development of human consciousness can lead to denigrating statements about indigenous perception, such as how the "mythicoreligious perspective" is "incompatible with an impersonal regard of objective reality."[13]

---

*Perhaps even more insidious is the "reductive operation" performed by the humanistic tradition, which seeks, in the words of James Hillman, to reduce the experience of a living cosmos to traits "that can become part of my wholeness. This is indeed 'growth'; but what grows is the ego. . . . Humanistic psychology affords a psychological technique with which humanism can wipe out the last trace of its ancient enemy, the Gods, from their last retreat in the soul. Ever since Protagoras, all modes of humanism have tried to maintain man in the center as the measure of all things. Now, by means of 'subjective interpretations' or 'Gestalt technique,' the first and immediate experience of the mythic . . . can be put into the human beings as traits and parts of his nature. So, this mode of interpretation becomes just one more modern way of inflating the ego. The ideas of wholeness and creative growth cover the old *hubris* of the hero" (*The Dream and the Underworld,* 104–5).

The simple, overlooked fact of the "mythicoreligious perspective" is that for cultures still rooted in the primal world, such as the Amazonian and Homeric, problem solving is predicated on a sentient cosmos. Classical scholars such as T. B. L. Webster have long observed that a "cornland can be the goddess Demeter, navigable water the god Okeanos, or a growing tree a nymph."[14]

Much as in the Amazon, where streams can be sentient and shamans can sing for the phlegm of the yacumama, the great boa constrictor of the water, to enter your body to heal it, Odysseus, shipwrecked and swimming for the Phaeacians' shore, can sense "the river's god and pray to him in spirit." Upon hearing Odysseus's prayers, the river god "stemmed his current, held his surge at once and smoothing out the swells before Odysseus now, drew him safe to shore" (*Odyssey* 5.489, 5.498–500).

Not only is the ocean teeming with sentience, the sky is also alive, as is seen when Telemachus, Odysseus's son, gets an instantaneous response to a question he poses: "At his last words, a bird flew past on the right, a hawk, Apollo's wind-swift herald—tight in his claws a struggling dove, and he ripped its feathers out . . ." As for the Koyukan, who assume "that nature is all aware, and that the sounds made by animals are at least as meaningful as those made by humans" and who "listen attentively to subtle nuances and variations in the calls of local birds,"[15] at this curious synchronicity, a prophet takes Odysseus's son aside and says, "Look, Telemachus, the will of the god just winged that bird on your right! Why, the moment I saw it, I knew it was a sign" (*Odyssey* 15.498–590, 15.594–97). Even Homer's metaphors can convey this symbiotic intimacy between the ancient Greeks and avian life. When Odysseus sheds his disguise as an old beggar and reveals himself to Telemachus, they fall into each other's arms and "cried out, shrilling cries, pulsing sharper than birds of prey—eagles, vultures with hooked claws" (*Odyssey* 16.246–47). Only those familiar with the haunting sounds of wild birds calling out to one another can appreciate how humane their voices really are!

A lovely, less martial example of avian-human communication is also from among the Koyukan people, where sometime in the past a horned owl was heard to clearly intone the words, "Black bears will cry"—an oracular pronouncement if ever there was one. Sure enough, the wild berries did not appear over the next two seasons, and the bears found it difficult to survive.[16]

Yet even for modern Westerners such experiences are not inaccessible. During the composition of this book, one night I stood in my living room window praying about an unexpected setback in a peyote ceremony. Looking out, I saw a deer, the animal manifestation of the peyote spirit, walking right down the middle of our road in the city of Oakland! In my five years of residence in this neighborhood, I have never seen a deer roam so far down from the hills above, nor have I spoken with a neighbor who has, either. My heart was immediately set at rest.

From these examples, among the plethora in ancient Greek texts, we can glimpse how a culture's communion with a living cosmos can bring valuable information or alter the environment in ways necessary for survival.

We can now ask this question: How is it that traditional, indigenous cultures—peoples who even now, after generations of flight deeper into the wild and pitched battle to survive the genocidal incursions of conquistadores and missionaries, and now the multinational oil, mining, and timber companies—might offer us an unprecedented view into the lifeways of ancient Indo-European cultures?

The answer to that question appears to lie somewhere in the deep strata of human consciousness, reaching back to and beyond the shamans of Paleolithic Europe who left traces of their thought life on the walls of the caves of Spain and France.

Somewhere in the earliest strata of our sixty-thousand-year-long experiment as *Homo sapiens* emerged what cultural historian Richard Tarnas describes as a "once universal mode of consciousness," where "reality is understood to be pervaded and structured by powerful numinous forces and presences that are rendered to the human imagination as the divinized figures and narratives of ancient myth."[17]

This primordial experience was enshrined in the Greek idea of *cosmos*—of the "real as an harmonious, all inclusive whole,"[18] which arose from the experience of the permeability of human consciousness to the sentience, the living presence, of the many dimensions of this world. As we saw above, such permeability is not just to the gods, but also to animals, plants, and insects, even ecological systems. All possess their own unique consciousness and participate in an order of meaning that transcends, and includes, human consciousness.

Following the first stirrings of modernity in the Middle Ages in the West, the gradually widening rupture between modern and native perception soon became acute. As philosopher Louis Dupré states, in a sudden, radical departure from tens of thousands of years of human culture, "The divine became relegated to a supernatural sphere separate from nature," and it "fell upon the human mind to interpret the cosmos, the structure of which had ceased to be given as intelligible."[19] Paradoxically, with this sudden onset of deafness, a new burst of creativity followed. Humanism, Copernicus's revelation of a Sol-centered planetary system, the idea of human progress, Descartes' *cogito ergo sum,* Shakespeare's *Hamlet*—all these are relics of this revolutionary move in the West to place human reason as the sole adjudicator of meaning. But such an arrogation of interpretive power, or, as C. S. Lewis wrote, "That great movement of internalization, and that consequent aggrandizement of man and desiccation of the outer universe, in which psychological history of the West has so largely consisted,"[20] was not without consequence. As the living, sentient nature of the cosmos waned in Western experience, the psyche closed like a flower and, as Dupré puts it, "Mental life separated from cosmic being."[21]

Numerous thinkers have proposed models to describe the consequences of this rupture. Richard Tarnas offers an elegant diagram to represent the differing psychic structure of the primal (indigenous) and modern minds (see figure 3.1 on page 42).

This rupture was exactly what J. R. R. Tolkien (whose *mythopoeic*— not mythological—approach is one of our great modern guides to awakening our indigenous mind) had in mind when he explained to C. S. Lewis:

You look at trees, he said, and called them "trees," and probably you do not think twice about the word. You call a star a "star," and think nothing more of it. But you must remember that these words, "tree," "star," were (in their original forms) names given to these objects by people with very different views from yours. To you, a tree is simply a vegetable organism, and a star simply a ball of inanimate matter moving along a mathematical course. But the first men to talk of "trees" and "stars" saw things very differently. To them, the world was alive with mythological beings. They saw the stars as living silver, bursting into flame in answer to the eternal music. They saw the sky as a jeweled tent, and the earth as the womb whence all living things have come. To them, the whole of creation was "myth-woven and elf patterned."[22]

In other words, such an aboriginal worldview is neither prerational nor delusional. It reflects a type of human inquiry that satisfies a desire for sophisticated interaction with the cosmos. As Tolkien also wrote, "The magic of Faery is not an end in itself, its virtue is in its operations: among these are the satisfaction of certain primordial human desires. One

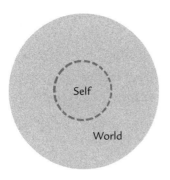

Primal Worldview

In the primal worldview, intelligence and soul (the shaded area) pervade all of nature and the cosmos, and a permeable human self directly particiaptes in that larger matrix of meaning and purpose within which it is fully embedded

Modern Worldview

In the modern worldview, all qualities associated with purposeful intelligence and soul are exclusively characteristic of human subject, which is radically distinct form the objective nonhuman world.

Fig. 3.1. Richard Tarnas's primal and modern worldviews

of these desires is to survey the depths of space and time. Another is to hold communion with other living beings."[23]

This desire to survey the depths of time and space is, of course, shared with the best of contemporary science, but differs in that primal perception involves direct apprehension by *seeing* its object of inquiry, rather than indirectly by analysis of that object. Among the best scientists, of course, these two modes are conjoined. Such was the case for Albert Einstein, who had the capacity, as his fellow physicists noted, to *see* underlying realities where they only perceived abstract formulas.[24]

As the model of the Hopi prophecy suggests, the emergence of these two roads has been a long time coming. Even in the *Odyssey,* we find that Alcinous, king of the Phaeacians, tells Odysseus a curious story, one that suggests the waning of indigenous perception was already underway at the time of Homer. The king confesses that, "The gods are working now in strange, new ways. Always, up to now, they came to us face-to-face whenever we'd give them grand, glorious sacrifices—they always sat beside us here and shared our feasts. Even when some lonely traveler meets them on the roads, they never disguise themselves. We're too close kin for that, close as the wild Giants are, the Cyclops too" (*Odyssey* 7.236–42).

Such a statement is reminiscent of a rueful comment I recently heard from a Native American at the end of a tipi ceremony: "Our ancestors could once speak with the animals, but we've lost that ability nowadays."

A similar example of this fading of permeable consciousness is the loss of vital connection to the directions, which for native peoples are sacred powers and are invoked in ceremonial contexts. How profound this inner orientation can be is seen, for example, among the Australian aboriginal speakers of the Guugu Yimithirr language, whose language simply has no egocentric coordinates at all. In order to convey location, the aborigines rely on the cardinal directions. Concepts such as *left* or *right, in front of* or *behind,* simply do not find expression in their thought or vocabulary. A speaker wishing to indicate where an object was left in your house would say, "I left it on the southern edge of the western table." Reportedly, the effect of their inner orientation results in a far less egocentric people: "If you saw a Guugu Yimithirr speaker pointing at himself, you would naturally assume he meant to draw attention to himself. In fact, he is pointing in the cardinal direction that happens to be behind his back. While we are always at the center of the world, and it would never occur to us that pointing in the direction of our chest could mean anything other than to draw attention to ourselves, a Guugu Yimithirr speaker points through himself, as if he were thin air and his own existence were irrelevant."[25]

A similar example of supernatural-seeming orientation comes from the Mayan people of Chiapas, Mexico. One speaker of Tzeltal "was blindfolded and spun around more than 20 times in a darkened house. Still blindfolded and dizzy, he pointed without hesitation at the geographical directions."[26]

Such deep attunement is usually credited, à la Whorf, to a language's structure imposing on its speakers a picture of reality; that is, speakers of Guugu Yimithirr have to be capable of performing "incredible feats of orientation"[27] because their language doesn't have a word for *right* or *left*. Yet from within the phenomenon of permeable consciousness, such a hypothesis sounds reductive and simplistic. It is equally plausible that indigenous peoples relate to the directions much as we do the force of gravity, as actual beings with an objective existence "out there."

Yet the wider perspective of the Hopi prophecy can allow us to add an additional touch to Tarnas's model. The disintegration of modernity offers new opportunities to free ourselves from the tyranny of official histories, from naively limited perspectives, and to evolve into culturally ambidextrous humans. Postmodernism has shown us that truth is porous, multidimensional, organic, rather than simply unmoored from absolute certainties, and can be held as simultaneously one and polyvalent, without falling into simpleminded cultural relativism. Like vegetation springing back up through widening cracks in the concrete, we now have an opportunity to step off the line of history and rejoin the cyclical process of the cosmos.

Inspired by the Hopi model, we can see a progression, like the rising and setting of the sun, if we simplify and expand Tarnas's model into a growth cycle (figure 3.2).

As the road of the two-hearted (which this work argues is analogous to the disintegrating trajectory of modernity) breaks up the possibility

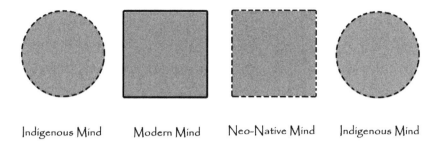

Indigenous Mind   Modern Mind   Neo-Native Mind   Indigenous Mind

Fig. 3.2. An expansion of Tarnas's model into a growth cycle

of going neo-native, achieving a synthesis between scientific and indigenous ways of knowing is now possible—as represented by the permeable square. Achieving such a balance of individual, rational consciousness and primal apprehension of a vital, living cosmos would not only safeguard the Earth and its future generations, but could lead to a renaissance of human culture and science. Finally, it may be our children's children will find their clans and become natives of the Earth once again. This does not mean a nostalgic retreat to the Americas of 1491 or Western Europe before the arrival of Christianity (although in many ways this wouldn't be a bad thing). Rather, as the Aboriginal speakers of Guugu Yimithirr are oriented to the directions, our descendents may know their relationship to, and location within, a living cosmos by instinctive dead reckoning.

A methodological question remains: How are we to approach the very ancient, traditional stories that appear in Homer's *Odyssey*? If they are neither factually true nor primitive delusion, what are they? How are we to interpret Alcinous's words and the other magical episodes of the poem?

The answer lies in the nature of the oral tradition itself, which has a dual function: to convey knowledge out of deep time and to *presence* the timeless realm in the here and now.

The first function is to communicate the accumulated wisdom of a people without recourse to what cognitive anthropologist Colin Renfrew calls "external symbolic storage," or literacy. Indeed, Renfrew credits writing with shaping the modern mind's style of cognition, for "theoretic thought . . . requires external symbolic storage."[28] Yet the theoretical capacity made possible by literacy also has a cost—it privileges abstractions over immediate reality: Orpheus could sing with the birds; Plato could not.

As described by philosopher David Abram, oral tradition uses story to encode crucial factual information into a compelling narrative—the most seaworthy of vehicles to be launched on the ocean of memory.

> Without writing, knowledge of the diverse properties of particular animals, plants, and places can be preserved only by being woven into *stories,* into vital tales wherein the specific characteristics of the plant are made evident through a narrated series of events and inter-actions. . . . And the more lively the story—the more vital or stirring the encounters within it—the more readily it will be in-corporated. . . . In this manner the character or personality of a medicinal plant will be easily remembered, its poisonous attributes will be readily avoided, and the precise steps in its preparation will be evident from the sequence of events in the very legend that one chants while pre-paring it. . . .
>
> In this light, that which literates misconstrue as a naïve attempt at causal explanation may be recognized as a sophisticated mne-monic method whereby precise knowledge is preserved and passed along from generation to generation.[29]

Certainly highly memorable episodes in the *Odyssey,* such as the battle with the Cyclops, the visit to Circe's palace, and the descent into Hades fit the bill as lively, dynamic, vital, and violent stories. In fact, the *Odyssey* is a treasure trove of oral tradition, much already very ancient by the age of the archaic Greeks. While Homer, as a *rhapsode,* wove the tapestry of his great song, his materials did not originate with him. Even with the newly emerged literary sensibility of the Homeric age, it is pos-sible to see how the stories retained much of their original oral encoding. In this way, the instructions Odysseus receives from Hermes to use the moly plant, "dangerous for a mortal man to pluck from the soil but not for deathless gods" (*Odyssey* 10.339–40), as a defense against the potion of Circe, may be understood as having once conveyed precise information of moly's medicinal virtue and preparation. Due to centuries of cultural drift, even in the age of Homer the instructions encoded by the story may have been indecipherable,* yet the essentially shamanic nature of the story is still easy to detect.

It is this particular feature of the oral tradition, therefore, that makes approaching Homer's text as an indigenous work, with its own messages out of deeper time, possible.

The second function of the oral tradition is of *presencing* that timeless realm through the medium of its retelling. As we shall see, the bards of Homer's age were not simply concerned with entertaining their audience or conveying information—they sought to open the pathways of inspired song to carry their audience into the experience of deep time.

When Homer invokes the Muse at the *Odyssey*'s beginning to "Sing for our time, too!" we can be confident it is not just a trope. He is shamanically calling for the power of the Muse to manifest herself through music and chant, to engage and even transform the psyche of the listeners by aligning them with archetypal events in mythic time and space. In this way the stories of oral tradition draw us back into deep memory, while simultaneously revealing their immanence in the here and now.

Homer, therefore, was the tip of the iceberg, an inheritor of a repertoire of prehistoric, indigenous folk tradition that he shaped for his time, under the influence of the mores of his culture and age. Yet there are imprints of older mythic cycles whose outlines can be detected in his work, like an original fresco over which generations of restorers have painted.

As the *Odyssey* stands poised in the history of consciousness between the native and the modern mind, we stand on our own threshold at modernity's waning, unable to see into the darkened landscape before us, uncertain where to place our next steps.

---

*Moly remains unidentified and the precise medicinal context in which it was used unknown. The best candidate is *Peganum harmala,* Syrian rue, which is identified as moly by the Roman physician Dioscorides. Ethnobotanist Dale Pendell comments that its "long and venerable reputation as an apotropaic certainly fits well with a plant that Homer might have known as a spell-breaker."[30]

As a threshold document and repository of oral tradition, the *Odyssey* provides a unique window into the origin of our contemporary ecological crisis. Just as did the ancient Hebrews in the oral tradition of our exile from the Garden of Eden, the ancient cultures of the Mediterranean told a story that violently dramatized the emerging break between indigenous and modern consciousness: the blinding of the Cyclops. As we shall see, if Odysseus is the first representative of modern human beings on literate humanity's horizon, he carries a profound curse for refusing to heal the indigenous Cyclops's eye. The consequence is the "ling'ring perdition, worse than any death" we have passed through in recent centuries, and are living out today.

It could also be that the tale of Odysseus shows us the way to reconcile our break with our native self, the way to put an end to our wanderings in history. In this way, it is truly a nostos, a homecoming song.

FOUR

RAPTUROUS SONG

Orpheus with his lute made trees
And the mountain tops that freeze,
Bow themselves when he did sing.
To his music plants and flowers
Ever sprung, as sun and showers
There made a lasting spring.
Everything that heard him play,
Even the billows of the sea
Hung their heads, and then lay by.
In sweet music is such art,
Killing care and grief of heart
Fall asleep, or hearing, die.

WILLIAM SHAKESPEARE

Oral tradition reaches unsuspected depths in the human soul through song. In the ancient Greek world, the highest aspiration of the poet/ singer was to be favored by the Muse with inspired song. Transformed into melody, the narrative had the capacity to enrapture the listener into the emotional depths and divine openings of a trance state. The singer became the channel of the living force of mythic time.

The power of song to induce a permeable state of consciousness is also present in the early Celtic and English literary traditions. For example, in the Irish mythological cycle, the poet Amergin summons the spirit of the land, the goddess Éire, through an inspired song that affirmed his communion, or symbiosis, with her, thus winning the island of Ireland for his people.

I am the wind that breathes upon the sea,
I am the wave of the ocean,
I am the murmur of the billows,
I am the ox of the seven combatants,
I am the vulture upon the rocks,
I am a beam of the sun,
I am the fairest of plants,
I am the wild boar in valor,
I am a salmon in the water,
I am a lake in the plain,
I am a word of science,
I am the point of the lance in battle,
I am the God who created in the head the fire.[1]

Becoming one with the spirit whose alliance is sought is one of the sacred pathways that embodied singing is able to sustain. The ancient Celts also knew the power of music to influence mood and consciousness, as it is shown in the story of the god Lugh. When Lugh first paid a visit to the court of Nuada, king of the Tuatha dé Danann, he took up the harp and began to play. "Plucking the strings gently and soothingly Nuada and his company fell into a peaceful sleep. When they awoke, Lugh played for them slow airs that made them weep. Then the music got faster and happier and, drying their tears, the whole company began to smile and laugh. Their laughter got louder and louder until the rafters rang with the sound."[2]

Intriguingly, the stages of trance that Lugh escorts his listeners through resemble the progression used by the Huichol Indians of Mexico, a culture with traditions as old as the ancient Celts. As Boyll related to me, during peyote ceremonies with the Huichol elder José Rios, listening to Rios's songs he found himself repeatedly progressing from deep isolation and sadness to ecstatic celebration within the space of a single evening. This progression turned out to be deliberately induced: Rios eventually explained to him that two modes of song are used in ceremonies. The first is the "mode of the orphan," which brings about forgetfulness, sleep, and the sorrow of an orphan. The second is the "mode of the flowers," which carries listeners to a consciousness of eternity, of joyous growth and expansion. This parallel suggests that Lugh's music may have been deliberately designed to direct the emotional experience of his listeners, another pathway into the permeability of human consciousness paved by inspired music and song. The human amnesiac condition here resolves into joyous remembrance, experientially elicited by this supernormal music as it retraces the mythic journey of the soul.

The literature of the early Celtic Christian tradition shows no lesser examples of the rapturous power of inspired song. In fact, the story of the first English poet celebrated by name, Caedmon, depicts one of the venues of song reception—dreams, also described by vegetalistas in the Peruvian Amazon when "receiving an icaro," or magic melody, from the spirit world, as we will see later. Moreover, this story tells us about the divine gift of song.

In the highly musical culture of the Celts, Caedmon, an Anglo-Saxon herdsman, sojourned around the year 650. According to the early church historian the Venerable Bede, the simple laborer often felt backward and inadequate around the Irish Christians: "Often at a drinking gathering, when there was an occasion of joy when all must in turn sing with a harp, when Caedmon saw the harp nearing him, he arose for shame from that feast and went home."[3]

One night, after quietly slipping out of another gathering, he went to tend the animals in the stables. There, "When he set his limbs at rest and fell asleep, some man stood by him in his dream and hailed and greeted him and addressed him by his name: 'Caedmon, sing me something.'"

Caedmon responded, "I do not know how to sing and for that reason I went out from this feast and went hither."

To which the figure responded, "Nevertheless, you must sing."

"What must I sing?" asked the bewildered Caedmon.

Said this mysterious figure, "Sing to me of the first Creation."

Caedmon then launched out in a fine blaze of song, with an erudition and musical intelligence that he had never known himself to possess. The next day, he described his dream to his foreman, who brought the event to the attention of the Abbess Hilda. Caedmon's gift was tested and confirmed when he composed and sang for her and her counselors, though never on the spot—Caedmon always had to dream first. Song reception, as described in a number of shamanic and spiritual traditions, seems to happen in moments of deep attunement or intimacy with the source of inspiration, which normally entails entry into a nonordinary state of consciousness or the permeable awareness of the dream state.

From this, and subsequent accounts, it is clear that he received a true initiation, for while he was widely imitated, his "poetic language adorned with the greatest sweetness and inspiration" could not be equaled, and caused many men and women to abandon worldly lives and take up the religious path. As the Venerable Bede concludes, it was "not through man that he songcraft learned, but he was divinely aided and through God's gift received the art of poetry."[4]

The association with the intrinsic power of a plant may also bring the gift of divinely inspired song, as we see in the account of a near contemporary of Homer. While tending his sheep at "the foothills of god-haunted Helikon," a sacred mountain of the Ancient Greeks on which two springs sacred to the Muses were located, Hesiod was accosted by the daughters of Zeus, the Muses, who trumpeted, "Listen, you country bumpkins, you swag-bellied yahoos, we know how to tell many lies that pass for truth, and we know, when we wish, to tell the truth itself." They then plucked a branch "from a laurel in full bloom" and gave it to him as a staff. After that, he says, they "breathed into me divine song."[5]

Why the Muses decided to grace a "swag-bellied yahoo" with the gift of song remains unclear in the account, yet, it is notable that the infusion of the gift happens upon reception of the laurel staff, the sacred tree whose leaves were chewed by the Oracle of Delphi to facilitate her entry into prophetic trance.

The reception of songs through association with, ingestion of, or intimate listening to medicinal plants seems to be a cross-cultural motif among indigenous healers. As her Ojibwe grandmother described to anthropologist Barbara Tedlock, in her society, "the ability to hear plants sing and converse with them is what defines a midé—a shaman, a person of spiritual power who heals with sacred plants."[6] Among vegetalistas of the Peruvian Amazon, the icaros, or magical melodies, "constitute the quintessence of shamanic power," and the most powerful icaros are considered to be those received "directly from the *madres* (spirit mothers) of the plants, frequently through dreams, visions, or auditory stimuli experienced during intensive 'diets' with the plants."[7]*

This is to say, the icaro *is* the energetic imprint of the plant spirit (animal, mineral, natural phenomenon, or divinity) that manifests in the healer's voice. Once an icaro has been bestowed, the healer can properly direct the intrinsic healing power of the plant to a client, even without the physical presence of the plant.

As we explored in the account of Nick's healing from a snakebite in chapter 2, healing in indigenous cultures involves the person's realignment with his or her relationships: with the inner self and with social and spiritual forces. From this perspective, we may say that the songs of the Greek bard, the inspired mystical singer, and the shaman are plucking different strings on the same lyre.

In Hesiod's account, this is expressed within the cosmovision of ancient Greece.

Blessed is the man whom the Muses love; sweet song flows from his mouth. A man may have some fresh grief over which to mourn, and

---

*These diets involve the periodic ingestion of the plant in the form of a brew, in conditions of isolation in the forest, in addition to strict dietary, sexual, and other environmental restrictions. When the diet is properly followed and the apprentice ready, the plant "dieted" grants its song, which "represent[s] a transference of the spirits of each plant, with all their knowledge and theriomorphic and anthropomorphic manifestations, into the body of the shaman."[8]

sorrow may have left him no more tears, but if a singer, a servant of the Muses, sings the glories of ancient men and hymns the blessed gods who dwell on Olympos, the heavy-hearted man soon shakes off his dark mood, and forgetfulness soothes his grief.[9]

This shaking off of dark moods by means of inspired song wasn't a momentary distraction—it appears to have come through attunement and reawakening to the greater life of the cosmos. This capacity was demonstrated by Hesiod's near contemporary, the philosopher Pythagoras, who performed "soul adjustments" with his music. Like Caedmon, Pythagoras worked with a particular divinity "through which he extended his powers of hearing, fixing his intellect on the sublime symphonies of the world, producing a melody fuller and more intense than anything effected by mortal sounds."[10] Susana's study on healing experiences attributed to icaros during traditional ayahuasca ceremonies* may shed light on Pythagorus's style of soul adjustment. It shows that, from the perspective of the listener, inspired singing reaches directly, intimately, and with utmost care to the core healing issue the person carries, touching a depth the person had not been able to experience otherwise. By means of the song, the person feels "seen," or "touched," or "sung" by a living, healing force other than themselves—an experience of communion that unveils an expanded and more genuine sense of themselves. Under the "spell" of the icaro, there is nothing else in the perceptual horizon but the singing and the inner experience unfolding in perfect attunement, as if locked in to one another. What follows is a chiropractic adjustment of the soul that realigns the listener with the cosmos and all his relations, as well as an integrative understanding of his health issues and concrete ways of addressing them.

As we know from Homer's descriptions of the bardic art, listeners to ancient singers didn't merely hear about divinities or past events, they experienced or relived them through the vision-provoking powers of the bard's voice. Yet, much like the listener, the singer herself is enraptured

---

*See Susana Bustos, "The Healing Power of Icaros: A Phenomological Study of Ayahuasca Experiences" (Ph.D. diss., California Institute for Integral Studies, 2008).

within the act of singing. Inspired singers seem to tap into something energetic woven into the fabric of creation. In an illustration of Caedmon on the cross at St. Mary's in Whitby, England, an angel is reaching down to touch his harp and a descending dove has just alighted on his head. These are now such familiar symbolic tropes for divine inspiration within the Christian tradition that we can miss the obvious: Caedmon is being played by creation, not the other way around.

Fig. 4.1. The Caedmon panel on the cross at St. Mary's in Whitby, England, located at the site of the Abbess Hilda's monastery, with its tropes of divine inspiration: the dove on the head and the angel touching the harp

If Caedmon's song was anything like the inspired strains of the ancient Greeks and those who still sing in the Amazon, it had the ineffable quality of *presencing* its subject: Caedmon didn't sing about the creation of the world, nor did he witness it. He sang the creation of the world anew.* As we shall see, Demodocus, the bard whose inspired song triggers a healing catharsis in Odysseus, demonstrates how "the privilege that Mnemosune [the goddess of memory] confers on the singer is that of a contact with the other world, the possibility of freely entering it and freely returning from it," for in this visionary state, "the past appears as a dimension of the Beyond."[11] In the ceremonial performances of bard and shaman alike, the singing becomes Ariadne's thread through the labyrinth.

Such simultaneous dwelling in multiple dimensions, as is required in the bardic art, has been noted by Brazilian anthropologist Pedro de Niemeyer Cesarino among singers in different South American cultures. Niemeyer Cesarino shows how their performances reflect the "scissioning" of the shaman's self, when his work requires engagement in actions simultaneously happening in alternate realities. Basically, the way the shaman constructs the lyrics allows a stereoscopic vision, a container for the multiple parallel experiences he is holding while performing the shamanic act.[12]

The *presencing* power of shamanic song may take yet another twist. Luis Eduardo Luna, the Ecuadorian anthropologist whose early studies helped introduce Peruvian vegetalismo to the outside world, writes about master healer don Manuel Cordova-Rios: "[Don Manuel] is able, through imitation, to bring visions of birds and animals to people so they are able to study their behavior. Through the icaros, the shaman is able to 'become one' with the animal and see the world accordingly."[13]

In other words, the *presencing* that shamanic songs may induce can go as deeply into the fabric of interconnectedness as to reveal realities with their own tenaciously independent ontological status, which interpenetrate

---

*This phenomenon reflects the widespread indigenous apprehension, as shown by Mircea Eliade, that human relationships with the eternal "paradigmatic models revealed to men in mythic time" need to be periodically regenerated through their reenactment or reliving in sacred time. In this way, the vitality of the origins of a culture continues to flow from its timeless source. (Eliade, *The Myth of the Eternal Return*, vii).

with our own. A fine illustration of the mysteriously empirical workings of shamanic song comes from a *curandero* in Chazuta, Peru, who leads ceremonies with the plant medicine *ayahuasca* for both locals and visiting Westerners.

In one ceremony, a Scottish woman, at the height of the vision-inducing effect of the brew, found herself in the living presence of a dragon, a mythical beast from her own native land. Synchronous with her unfolding vision, sitting in the darkness across the room from her, the unsuspecting shaman found himself beholding an animal he had never seen before: a gigantic, fire-breathing serpent with wings. Awestruck, he burst into song, even as Caedmon once did, receiving the fully formed icaro of the dragon that both mediated its power into the ceremony and accompanied the Scottish woman's experience in perfect syntony.

Some shamans even claim to "'understand' the language of certain animals,"[14] in the old European sense in which Sigurd, having tasted the blood of the dragon, could understand the language of birds and animals.

Shakespeare and Tolkien both knew of the *presencing* capacity of song. Both of Shakespeare's final plays, *The Tempest* and *Henry VIII,* reveal his thought turning toward the rapturous power of music.

In *Henry VIII*, Katherine of Aragon, the dying wife of King Henry, calls to a serving woman, "Take thy lute, wench. My soul grows sad with troubles; Sing, and disperse 'em if thou canst" (3.1.1–2), echoing the wisdom of Hesiod that upon hearing inspired music, "the heavyhearted man soon shakes off his dark mood."

The young woman sings an invocation to Orpheus, an ancient bard whose song was of such shamanic potency it stirred nature to growth, calmed the sea, and tamed wild animals—as well as resurrecting the dead. Concluding, she sings:

> *In sweet music is such art,*
> *Killing care and grief of heart*
> *Fall asleep, or hearing, die. (Henry VIII 3.1.12–14)*

This transport into the living heart of a sacred song that the serving girl sings, so akin to sleep or death, is soon realized in a subsequent scene of the play, as Katherine, now dying, asks her musicians to play so she may sit "meditating on that celestial harmony I go to" (*Henry VIII* 4.2.79–80). As they play, she has a dream vision of the coming of "six personages, clad in white robes, wearing on their heads garlands of bays," who bow to her, dance, and crown her with the garland of bay leaves two by two. Katherine makes signs of rejoicing, and the spirits then vanish, taking the garland with them.

Awakening, the queen sighs, "Spirits of peace, where are ye?" Turning to her counselors, she asks, "Saw you not, even now, a blessed troop invite me to a banquet, whose bright faces cast thousand beams upon me, like the sun?" (*Henry VIII* 4.2.83–84, 87–89).

But the vision has faded. Her counselors stare blankly at her, uncomprehending. In dismay she cries out, "Are ye all gone, and leave me here in wretchedness behind ye?" (*Henry VIII* 4.2.83–84) Commanding her musicians to cease their wooden sawing on their instruments, she declares their earthly strains are now "harsh and heavy to me" (4.2.95).

Encountering this mystical sequence, embedded in the midst of an otherwise lackluster historical drama, one cannot but wonder what Shakespeare's final years were disclosing to him about the power of music over consciousness.

J. R. R. Tolkien, whose mythopathic imagination reintroduced many of the characteristics of the indigenous mind back into the Western imagination, depicted the effect of such inspired song in *The Lord of the Rings*, which, like the *Odyssey*, could be called an inspired song itself.

In Rivendell, the house of Elrond where living memory of the blessed lands across the sea is still preserved, Frodo experiences the enchanting power of elvish song, whose transporting power resembles that which arises from the Homeric bard's invocation of the Muse, daughter of Mnemosune, where, "What the poet prays for is not just an accurate memory—for this, though highly necessary, would be memory only of an inaccurate *kleos* [renown, fame, or glory as preserved in mere human memory]—but an actual vision of the past to supplement the kleos. Such visions, welling up from the unknown depths of the mind, must once have been felt as something immediately 'given,' and because of its immediacy more trustworthy than oral tradition."[15]

> At first the beauty of the melodies and of the interwoven words in elven tongues, even though he understood them little, held him in a spell, as soon as he began to attend to them. Almost it seemed the words took shape, and visions of far lands and bright things that he had never yet imagined opened out before him; and the firelit hall became a golden mist above seas of foam that sighed upon the margins of the world. Then the enchantment became more and more dreamlike, until he felt that an endless river of swelling gold and silver was flowing over him, too multitudinous for its pattern to be comprehended; it became part of the throbbing air about him, and it drenched and drowned him. Swiftly, he sank under its shining weight into a deep realm of sleep.[16]

What Frodo doesn't fully apprehend about "enchantment" Tolkien explains elsewhere, for like icaros and other transporting song, "If you are present at a Faërian drama you yourself are, or think that you are, bodily inside its Secondary world. The experience may be very similar to dreaming . . . but in Faërian drama you are in a dream that some other mind is weaving, and the knowledge of that alarming fact may slip from your grasp."[17] Intensified consciousness, for Tolkien, is a potion too strong for the ordinary mode of apprehension. Like the dragon manifesting in the Scottish woman's ayahuasca ceremony, we are swallowed up in it. We "give to it Primary Belief, however marvelous the events."[18]

Such is the Fellowship's experience inside Lothlórien, the Dreamflower, which exists like an isle outside of time in the landscape of Middle Earth. "When Sam, in Lórien, says he feels as if he is 'inside a song,' we take as metaphor what Tolkien means as a hidden reality. Sam is in truth inside a song, an artistic creation woven by another mind,"[19] that is, the Lady Galadriel.

Yet perilous as Tolkien knew a sojourn inside the realm of song to be, its restorative effect on the company is marked—such is this catalytic power of healing and reception of knowledge outside of ordinary time.

The true age of the bardic art is unknown, yet some indication of its age can be gleaned from a Cycladic sculpture of a seated bard, a lyre on one knee and a geometrically stylized head thrown back in what is clearly the rapt transport of song, dated to 2300 BCE.

Fig. 4.2. This figure, created by the culture that flourished 1,500 years before the recording of the Odyssey, could be an image of Homer himself, "launching out in a fine blaze of song."

Such time depth points to the shamanic roots of the bardic art. By the time of Homer, the professions of seer and poet had become distinct, yet their common inspiration was still acknowledged and we can imagine that the most accomplished among them would combine elements of both professions. Certainly we witness this capacity in Homer's Demodocus, along with a third shamanic characteristic: like a good Hippocratic physician, for whom "the healing art involves a weaving of a knowledge of the gods into the texture of the physician's mind,"[20] Demodocus's song has the ability to awaken the *physis*,* the innate healing capacity of the body/mind, which had the power to rebalance itself at its moment of crisis.

This therapeutic power of bardic song, called *aphthiton,* or "imperishable," by Homer, has strong associations with vital liquids or substances that give and restore life, especially the vitality of plant life. Gregory Nagy depicts aphthiton as denoting "an *unfailing stream* of water, fire, semen, vegetal extract," which gives bardic song its capacity to "counter the decay to which mortal things are subject."[21]

The concept of aphthiton has an underlying affinity with the vegetalista's notion of the magical powers of the icaros. These melodies invoke, distill, and communicate the mariri, or spiritual essence, of the life-giving plants that have formed healing (or hexing) alliances with the shaman. The intrinsic knowledge or power of this spiritual essence is transferred to a person or object by means of the singing. Thus, the infusion of the mariri of the plant chacruna, for example, whose spirit is seen as the queen of the forest and whose consciousness runs through all the waterways beneath and through the jungle canopy, gives visionary insight into the complex and subtle knowledge of the rain forest itself. The icaro of the chiric sanango, an epiphytic strangler vine, instills the power to confront issues of lack of integrity and to release deep fears.

The bard's visionary capacity and ability to receive promptings from

---

*Homer only uses the word *physis* once throughout his entire corpus, in the episode where Hermes explains the medicinal virtue of the plant moly, where physis is translated as "nature." Odysseus relates, "Hermes showed me all its name and nature" (*Odyssey* 10.337).

the Muse, then, point to a common praxis with the shaman who uses the voice to guide the psyche of his or her clients. Certainly, ceremonies with the plant brew ayahuasca, normally conducted in the darkness of the jungle night, cast the shaman in the ancient role of psychopomp, a guide of souls into the realm of the dead, dream, and myth.

The mysterious power of the bard's voice is demonstrated more than once in the *Odyssey,* but nowhere more memorably or clearly as in the catharsis Odysseus undergoes in the hall of the Phaeacians, where he finally escapes the death grip of Poseidon's water realm.

There we encounter Demodocus, the "faithful bard the Muse adored above all others, true, but her gifts were mixed with good and evil both: she stripped him of sight but gave the man the power of stirring, rapturous song" (*Odyssey* 8.73–76). We see him led into the banquet hall, set in a silver-studded chair, where Demodocus, inspired by the Muse, immediately zeroes in on the presence of Odysseus. When he reaches for his lyre, he takes up the theme of "the strife between Odysseus and Achilles, Peleus' son." Suddenly confronted with his own kleos among men, Odysseus, who for a decade had not heard a single human voice other than his long-lost shipmates', is struck to the quick.

> *Clutching his flaring sea-blue cape*
> *in both powerful hands, drew it over his head*
> *and buried his handsome face,*
> *ashamed his hosts might see him shedding tears.*
> *Whenever the rapt bard would pause in the song,*
> *he'd lift the cape from his head, wipe off his tears*
> *and hoisting his double-handled cup, pour it out*
> *to the gods. (Odyssey 8.100–106)*

Odysseus, moved by Demodocus's song, later sends him an offering, stating, "From all who walk the earth our bards deserve esteem and awe, for the Muse herself has taught them paths of song. She loves the breed of harpers" (*Odyssey* 8.538–40). Finally approaching the bard, Odysseus praises him and makes a request that comes cloaked as a challenge: he wishes to hear, with even more intimacy, the cathartic power of the bard's voice.

> *I respect you, Demodocus, more than any man alive—*
> *surely the Muse has taught you, Zeus's daughter,*
> *or god Apollo himself. How true to life,*
> *all too true . . . you sing the Achaeans' fate . . .*
> *as if you were there yourself or heard it from one who was.*
> *But come now, shift your ground. Sing of the wooden horse*
> *Epeus built with Athena's help, the cunning trap that*
> *Good Odysseus brought one day to the heights of Troy,*
> *Filled with fighting men who laid the city waste.*
> *Sing that for me—true to life as it deserves—*
> *And I will tell the world at once how freely*
> *The Muse gave you the gods' own gift of song. (Odyssey*
>   8.546–58)

Demodocus, stimulated by Odysseus, launches into "a fine blaze of song," *presencing,* with his capacity to access the past as a dimension of the Beyond, the experience of the Trojan Horse and the battle within the walls of Troy that followed.

> *He sang how troops of Achaeans broke from cover,*
> *streaming out of the horse's hollow flanks to plunder*
>   *Troy—*
> *he sang how left and right they ravaged the steep city,*
> *sang how Odysseus marched right up to Deiphobus' house*
> *like the god of war on attack with diehard Menelaus.*
> *There, he sang, Odysseus fought the grimmest fight*
> *he had ever braved but he won through at last,*
> *thanks to Athena's supernatural power. (Odyssey*
>   8.577–84)

In this remarkable feat, Demodocus sets Odysseus's experiences in the center of his narrative as if he were Odysseus himself. Much like the experience of falling under the spell of an icaro, where "the client enters a state where the sense of self feels locked into deep absorption in the singing and the concomitant display of visions, organic sensations, emotions and thoughts, all unfolding together in perfect syntony,"[22] Odysseus relives his own experiences at Troy locked in the spell of Demodocus's voice.

Stung to the quick, after a decade's struggle to escape his entrapment in the watery realm of Poseidon, Odysseus is able to release the long-pent-up grief he has carried for years. Groaning, with labored breathing, "Great Odysseus melted into tears, running down from his eyes to wet his cheeks" (Odyssey 8.586–87).

A glimpse of his inner experience is given by Homer, suggesting that Demodocus's song is awakening the physis, the innate healing capacity within Odysseus, for he weeps:

> As a woman weeps, her arms flung round her darling
>   husband,
> a man who fell in battle, fighting for town and
>   townsmen,
> trying to beat the day of doom from home and children.
> Seeing the man go down, dying, gasping for breath,
> she clings for dear life, screams and shrills—
> but the victors, just behind her,
> digging spear-butts into her back and shoulders,
> drag her off in bondage, yoked to hard labor, pain,
> and the most heartbreaking torment wastes her cheeks.
>   (Odyssey 8.588–96)

This is no mere metaphor—such intense catharsis is described nowhere else in Homer. Odysseus has been flung into an experience of "profound intimacy with oneself and the singing,"[23] for, as popular historian Thomas Cahill points out, "In the *Iliad,* the worst opprobrium that one hero can hurl at another is to call him a 'woman.'"[24] Yet here, "the unthinkable has come to pass: Odysseus has become Andromache."[25]

Odysseus the famous sacker of cities, has come to identify experientially not only with a warrior's despised feminine nature, but even with the very women he once took captive.

Is this the remedy that Odysseus required in order to finally depart from Poseidon's realm? Does the battle-hardened warrior, in order to return to the human realm, have to embody, in a feminine consciousness, the immense depths of suffering caused by war?

That may be so, especially if it is correct that the root of *nostos,* as the homecoming song of the *Odyssey* was called, "implies a return of consciousness (*noos*) in a 'coming back' from Hades."[26] The song of Demodocus is calling Odysseus back from his sojourn in the land of the dead.

Just as Demodocus provokes a cathartic outpouring of grief in Odysseus by allowing him to relive his past, the ancient physician sought a medicine that would provoke "a symptomology like that of the disease."[27]

Again, the parallels with experiences of intense healing with icaros are striking. There, the patient experiences "being touched in his core healing issue with a depth, care and precision he has never experienced before," and under the spell of the shaman's voice, "the body experiences a release of old habits and patterns, and they restructure into wider and more flexible ways of being in the world."[28] This is the therapeutic effect Odysseus appears to undergo, for his catharsis marks the moment he breaks free from his vexed journey through the watery realm of the unconscious and its endless plethora of gods.*

Demodocus's restructuring song enables Odysseus to reclaim his human identity and reintegrate into the human realm—which he realizes that very evening and all through the night by recounting the story of his journey for the spellbound Phaeacians. No doubt he sang it, accompanying himself on the lyre.

---

*The ancient philosopher Heraclitus, whom James Hillman, in his book *The Dream and the Underworld,* dubs the first depth psychologist, left these fragments indicating the deep affinity of death with water: "To souls it is death to become water" and "It is delight, or rather death, to souls to become wet."

FIVE

THE PLANT GODDESS CIRCE

Not all those who pass
In front of the Great Mother's chair
Get past with only a stare.
Some she looks at their hands
To see what sort of savages they were.

GARY SNYDER

Early on in the *Odyssey* we see Helen, daughter of Zeus, slipping a curious potion called nepenthe into a mixing bowl for wine: "Heart's ease, dissolving anger, magic to make us all forget our pains. . . . No one who drank it deeply, mulled in wine, could let a tear roll down his cheeks that day, not even if right before his eyes some enemy brought down a brother or darling son with a sharp bronze blade. So cunning the drugs that Zeus's daughter plied" (*Odyssey* 4.245–52).

Helen then picks up a harp to entertain her visitors with songs, which suggests that bardic performances may have been enhanced by psychotropic ingredients in the refreshments.[1] Such a marvelous brew illustrates that ancient wine "did not contain alcohol as its sole inebriant but was ordinarily a variable infusion of herbal toxins in a vinous liquid. Unguents, spices, and herbs, all with recognized psychotropic properties, could be added,"[2] allowing for a potency more fitting to ancient descriptions of

66

wine's effects. Pendell draws the connection between Helen's Egyptian source for the recipe of nepenthe and the historical fact that Thebes was famous for its poppy fields. He goes on to speculate, "Nepenthe was probably a mixture, perhaps *mekonium* in wine, with mandrake and henbane. Tropanes go well with opium."[3]

Such an episode is only one among many in the *Odyssey* where plants play mind-altering and magical roles characteristic of native cultures with plant-based shamanic traditions. Telemachus's encounter with the semidivine Helen's potion is only a mild example of the potent art, compared to the shamanic showdown of magical plants to take place in the island palace of Circe. There we can understand Circe's dramatic wooing of Odysseus as shamanic, bearing as it does the deep archetypal stamp of the symbiotic relationship between plant, spirit ally, and shaman.*

The tale of Circe's transformation of Odysseus's crew members into swine, and their subsequent rescue by Odysseus, aided by the sacred plant moly, is among the most famous episodes in the *Odyssey,* yet the resonances and lineaments of divine figures within the tale have far greater time depth than is generally recognized.

Odysseus and his men, the story goes, arrive on Circe's island after their narrow escape from a Cyclops. Investigating the isle, Odysseus's men approach a palace set on a hill, surrounded by friendly lions and wolves that fawn and swish their tails around them, giving the men the jitters. They are then drawn by a woman's spellbinding song to enter the palace hall, where they behold Circe, the goddess, weaving on her loom. Arising, she welcomes them, and, inviting them to a banquet, gives them wine into which she famously stirs "wicked drugs to wipe from their memories any thought of home" (*Odyssey* 10.260). Striking the men with her wand, she turns them into swine. She then drives them into a sty, flinging in acorns and mast for them to eat.

---

*Classical scholars have long suspected shamanism at work in the clash between Circe and Odysseus. For example, *Bloom's Guides: The Odyssey* comments, "There is something shamanistic about this episode" (Bloom, *Bloom's Guides,* 55). Yet as far as I know, no classical scholar has yet to investigate what that "something" might be through study of the ethnography of shamanistic cultures.

Fig. 5.1. Circe and the swine man.

Elpennor, who is distrustful, has lingered outside to watch the proceedings and hastens back to report to Odysseus. Odysseus grimly sets off to Circe's palace, alone, clueless about how to rescue his men. Along the way he encounters Hermes manifesting in the vicinity of a sacred plant, a powerful antidote that can protect him from Circe's magic—the moly we have discussed before. Carefully instructing him on how to counteract Circe's spells and win her as an ally, Hermes pulls up the plant by the roots and gives it to Odysseus.

Thus immunized to Circe's magic, Odysseus then enters her hall and allows her to seat him and feed him her potion. When it has no effect on him, Odysseus rushes her with his sword and, cowering, Circe recognizes him as Odysseus, who Hermes had prophesied to her would one day arrive on her isle. She then invites him to her bed, promising that she won't unman him. Circe then restores Odysseus's men, and they enjoy a yearlong supernatural feast with her, in which their haggard spirits are restored and their strength renewed for the rest of their voyage.

The virtue of animal *becoming* is a theme we will return to in our next chapter, but for now we can ask, What plant could Circe have used to wreak such a profound transformation on Odysseus's men? According to Pendell, "the Greeks knew mandrake well, sometimes calling it 'Circe's plant,' and it would be a most suitable candidate for turning men into swine."[4] Mandrake is a member of that tropane alkaloid–packed Solanaceae family, which also gives us that long list of fabled ingredients of witch's lore: datura, jimsomweed, henbane, belladonna, and, of course, tobacco. Like her niece, Medea, who rescues Jason with her magic potions, Circe is a *pharmakeus,* a term that Robert Fagles translates as "witch," who mixes *kaka pharmaka,* "wicked drugs," and as such she is the ancestor of the modern pharmacist.

Circe is no mere sorceress or *bruja,* however. We can better understand her nature as the confluence of oral tradition around two ancient feminine divinities, which flowed into the storytelling repertoire of the ancient Greeks from shoals of time as distant as the early Paleolithic.

Her first characteristic appears to have come through the high culture of Crete, where her divinity was inextricably interwoven with plant sentience. From an enthnographic perspective, Circe has strong features of a resident divinity of a magical plant.

Her second characteristic is as the *potnia theron,* the mistress of animals. This divinity is of great time depth* and appears in both masculine and feminine forms. Her house is located in the wilds, and within it she keeps and releases the souls of the animals. It is with her that the shaman must bargain for the game to sustain his people, and it is she who receives human souls in exchange.

---

*As we shall see, German philologist Walter Burkert argues the Cyclops's tale in the *Odyssey* has deep structural analogues with other violent shamanic negotiations with the master of animals, and that it concludes as well with the release of the animals (in the form of the Cyclops's rustled herd). Odysseus's clash with Circe and his rescue and freeing of his men follow a similar pattern, although with an even more shamanic twist: he releases from captivity the imprisoned souls of his men, constrained to dwell within the bodies of beasts.

CIRCE AS RESIDENT PLANT DIVINITY

Accustomed as urban dwellers now are to manufactured drugs, we have become culturally distanced from the total experience of immersion into plant "consciousness" known by our ancestors. Coca, a plant held sacred by the indigenous people of the Andes, has flooded our marketplaces in the form of its derivative, cocaine. The opium poppy, held sacred throughout the ancient world, is now experienced primarily through its derivatives, heroin and morphine. While these powerful drugs can, when intelligently used, have beneficial effects, they don't carry that characteristic of beneficent sentience that plant medicines taken in a traditional manner have, nor are they generally received with the same profound gratitude and veneration expressed by native peoples.

Jane Straight, a cultivator of medicinal plants, described the effect of a treatment of a strong tea made solely of dried opium poppy heads when she had thrown out her back. "I was in agony," she said, when a friend found her crawling on the ground. Once situated in a warm, safe location, she drank an "elixir" of opium.

> The *Papaver somniferum* spirit lovingly caressed me into her cloud of sweet dreams, creating a safe haven for me to leave my body. That's when the real healing began. I could no longer feel any physical sensation and relaxed completely, allowing gravity to realign my spine. I lay there for what seemed a blissful eternity while the opium spirit dusted every cell with clear light. It was an extraordinary experience that left me feeling extremely refreshed.[5]

It is little wonder that ancient peoples posited a divine personality manifesting through such powerful plants as opium. Whether indigenous peoples are correct that plants actually possess a form of sentience is almost a moot point in light of the power of such an experience. Yet without an intimate, even loving, relationship among the healer, plant, and patient, such beneficial outcomes are rare.

Comical outcomes may even result. Consider, for example, the curious anecdote given by E. R. Dodds in his *The Greeks and the Irrational* about a certain Dr. Oesterreich, a classicist who once investigated the psychoactive properties of the laurel leaves ingested by the Oracle of Delphi, whose fame at one time extended throughout the Hellenic world. The laurel tree, of course, is sacred to Apollo, ever since his love, Daphne, was transformed into one while under his hot, amorous pursuit. Its branches and leaves may have been used in a ritual manner, according to some contemporary reports, to induce the trance states of the oracle.

It appears the professor disregarded historical accounts of the ritual used to approach the god's seat, as well as any anthropological accounts of oracular plant practice he might have been able to procure. Instead, he simply sat down and, like a good ungulate, "chewed a large quality of laurel leaves in the interests of science." Unsurprisingly, he was "disappointed to find himself no more inspired than usual."[6]

One can imagine an ancient pharmakeus shaking her head, asking, "Why should Apollo permit such a barbarian to enter into His mysteries?"

As ethnobotanist Kate Harrison explains, while there "are many approaches to recognizing this 'plant spirit' in different indigenous cultures, all are characterized by an attitude of deep reverence." In a way analogous to the mushroom, whose real vegetal being can extend for miles underground, the plant is only the visible aspect of a much greater being. Indigenous cultures "view each species as possessing a distinct spirit or of being a spirit that has dressed itself in matter and taken on a certain form and appearance and chemical signature. All of these approaches recognize the importance of talking to and listening to these plants and asking their permission to be used as medicine."[7]

As well, the potency of a plant may lie in "the physical plant itself, or the physical plant as a substrate of magical power, or the spirit of the plant, acting independently of the physical plant."[8]

The mystery of human-vegetal communion goes deep in many indigenous cultures, whose relationship with plants extends back generations and is inextricably bound up with their cosmology. Contemporary Mohawk medicine woman Katsi Cook illustrates the crucial importance of approaching plant medicines with appropriate ritual.

As a midwife, when I ask a mother to begin to use, say, slippery elm, there's a whole protocol to be followed, I have to find an elder of our community who's going to fix that medicine for her, because it isn't just about stripping the inner bark from a live tree. It involves the right approach to the tree, the proper respect and address to the tree. For instance, in addressing a plant, you must use your Mohawk name, gained through birth into a clan such as Turtle, Bear or Wolf, and given to you in ceremony to establish the proper relationship of each individual child to the natural world, including the medicine plants.[9]

As the great ethnobotanist Richard Evans Schultes summed up this phenomenon: "Shamanism depends in great part on the supernatural powers resident in certain plants. These resident divinities are organic chemical constituents that allow mortal man to communicate through visual, auditory and other hallucinations with the spirit world."[10]

As all of these testimonies emphasize, one must first recognize and know the proper address in order to commune with the divinity available within plants.

What is the evidence, then, that the goddess with whom Odysseus establishes a sexually ecstatic, healing, and divinatory relationship references this experience of plant sentience?

The Homeric Greeks carried within their collective psyche a strong memory of the legendary Cretan island culture of a thousand years earlier, a society whose strong matriarchal elements had infused their own with strange echoes of divinities and superior culture. It is still inexplicable how none of the palaces excavated by Sir Arthur Evans on Crete showed any sign of defenses. In contrast to the palaces of the patriarchal Mycenaeans with their extensive defensive structures and martial symbolism on the Greek mainland, the palaces of the Cretans celebrated nature and the feminine, were open to the elements, and enjoyed indoor plumbing, among other refinements—all of which may have struck the Mycenaean mind as mysterious, if not ominous.

With this combination of awe and fear we find Odysseus and his men approaching the island halls of the goddess Circe. From deep inside her palace, they "heard her singing, lifting her spellbinding voice as she glided back and forth at her great immortal loom, her enchanting web a shimmering glory only goddesses can weave" (*Odyssey* 10.242–45).

Much like the sirenas of the Amazon, who originally came from the deep waters of Lake Titicaca to teach the art of weaving to the Incas, Circe's song enchants Odysseus's men, who declare, "How she sings—enthralling! The whole house is echoing with her song. Goddess or woman—let's call out to her now!" (*Odyssey* 10.249–51).

Circe is also very dangerous—she is a plant sorceress/divinity whose voice transmits intoxicating power. This ancient motif, arising out of indigenous experience, is still a living tradition among inheritors of a shamanic tradition as ancient as Homer's,* the Huichol Indians of Mexico, among whom it occurs in relation to the plant solandra. This plant, which belongs to the same Solanaceae family as mandrake, is known among the Huichol as the sorcerer Kieri.

For the initiated, the Kieri is approached indirectly, by consuming the honey of the bees that visit the plant.† For the uninitiated, "with the enchanting music of his violin [Kieri] lures the unwary and bids them taste of his leaves, his flowers, his roots and his seeds. Whoever obeys his wiles suffers insanity or death."[11] Not only that, like Odysseus's men, they can undergo animal transformation and require rescue by a shaman with a more powerful spirit ally, as Odysseus must do with the aid of Hermes: "People bewitched by Kieri will believe themselves to be birds, for example, able to fly to the highest rocks, unless they are saved by a shaman with the aid of peyote and Kauyumarie, they will dash themselves to death below."[12]

---

*A snuffing pipe from the ancient Mesoamerican city of Monte Albán, shaped in the form of a deer holding a peyote cactus in his mouth, has been dated to around 2,500 years of age, nearly contemporary with Homer. (See Peter Furst's book, *Hallucinogens and Culture*).

†See Jay Fikes's *The Man Who Ate Honey* for the story of the boyhood initiation of Huichol shaman Jesús González Mercado, who found himself initiated by the Kieri spirit after eating a honeycomb saturated with Kieri pollen.

An enrapturing goddess was once very familiar, both to the Cretans and to the mainland Mycenaeans who fought at Troy. Although no written records exist, the archaeologist's spade has turned up numerous representations of her as the "goddess of poppies, patroness of healing."[13] One of her best-known terra-cotta figures, a bare-breasted goddess with upraised arms, was found in a secret room of a rural cult house on Crete from the same period as the Trojan War. Adorning her headdress are poppy capsules, stained brown like opium, which clearly display five to six vertical notches in the capsule skin—the time-honored method of extracting the opium sap. Notable as well is the expression of transport on the figurine's face, "giving her the appearance of being in a state of torpor induced by opium. For this reason, the archaeologist who discovered her proposed that she should be called the 'goddess of ecstasy.'"[14] Surrounding her was evidence that her worship was cultic: "the remnants of a heap of coal on the ground in the room where the goddess was found provide further evidence that the opium was taken by the inhalation of vapours, probably for psychotropic purposes."[15]

Fig. 5.2. The opium goddess of Crete

This cult of the ecstatic goddess also reached the mainland Greeks. Discovered in the Acropolis of Mycenae was a golden ring of exquisite craftsmanship, depicting a female deity receiving "an offering of three opium capsules, surrounded by cult Cretan symbols like the double axe, with the sun and moon above and seated under a tree. This shows the goddess must be associated with the worship of trees, therefore of nature and fertility."[16]

"Tree worship" seems an awkward explanation for this scene of the opium goddess sitting enthroned amid her panoply of the natural world. One suspects we are getting a glimpse into the opium pure land, instead.

Fig. 5.3. The enthroned opium goddess

Such an evocation of the healing power of the plant goddesses is characteristic of the icaros, which are even now sung in the Amazon, such as this invocation that opens ayahuasca ceremonies at Takiwasi, the center for the treatment of addiction in Tarapoto, Peru:

Madre Ayahuasca	Mother Ayahuasca
Llévame hasta el sol	Carry me toward the sun
De la savia de la tierra	From the nectar of the earth

Hazme beber . . .	Make me drink . . .
Llévame contigo hacia el sol	Bring me with you toward the sun
Del sol interior hacia arriba	From the sun within toward the sky
Hacia arriba subiré, madre	Toward the sky I will rise, mother
Úsame, háblame, enséñame	Use me, speak to me, teach me
Enséñame a ver . . .	Teach me to see . . .
A ver al Hombre dentro del hombre	To see the Man inside the man
A ver el Sol dentro y fuera del hombre	To see the Sun within and without the man
Usa mi cuerpo	Use my body
Hazme brillar	Make me shine
Con brillo de estrellas	With the light of the stars
Con calor del sol	With the heat of the sun
Con luz de luna y fuerza de tierra	With the light of the moon and the power of the earth

Within the orbit of the opium experience is another feature that associates it with divinity: a sense of a blissful eternity spent outside the harsh confines of the mechanism of time, a healing gift to mortals, experienced as communion with the immortal nature of the goddess that the plant manifests in this world. In fact, so pervasive was the symbol of the poppy in Cretan culture, it is thought that the "various narcotic substances it contains were considered symbols of immortality."[17]

Of course, such intoxication has its perils. As we know from the history of opium smoking and laudanum drinking—and later heroin, morphine, and oxycodone addiction—it is possible to get trapped in her orbit. After Circe diagnoses Odysseus and his men as "burnt-out husks, your spirits haggard, sere, always brooding over your wanderings long and hard, your hearts never lifting with any joy—you've suffered far too much" (*Odyssey* 10.509–12), she engulfs them in a timeless state of ease, where they sit, "day in, day out . . . feasting on sides of meat and drafts of heady wine." Finally, "when the year was gone and seasons wheeled by and the months waned and the long days came round again," Odysseus's crew members arouse him with cries of, "Captain, this is madness! High time you thought of your own home at last" (*Odyssey* 10.516–21). But, of course, they are then thoroughly recuperated and ready to move back into the struggle for existence in the field of time.

CIRCE AS POTNIA THERON

Another feature of Circe, characteristic of many indigenous cosmologies, is her kinship with the potnia theron, the mistress of animals. According to Burkert, "The idea of a Master or Mistress of the Animals who must be won over to the side of the hunters is widespread and very possibly Paleolithic in origin; in the official religion of the Greeks this survives at little more than the level of folklore."[18]

Yet folklore is a vital force indeed. We are reminded of this indigenous relationship of reciprocity and gratitude between hunter and prey in a brief hunting episode just before the discovery of Circe's palace, in which Odysseus says, "A god took pity on me, wandering all alone; he sent me a big stag with high branching antlers, right across my path" (*Odyssey* 10.172–74). While the cosmology of the hunt was fading in importance for the Mycenaean Greeks, we can see the primal ethos intact in Odysseus's account.

That unknown god is about to reveal herself to Odysseus and his men.

Different indigenous peoples identify this god as the master of animals, who releases and withholds the animals. The caribou-hunting Labrador Eskimos and Innus believe in the "King of the Caribou who gave the caribou [reindeer] to the hunters. They believed also that they would not appear unless the hunters showed them proper respect."[19] For the Eskimos

Fig. 5.4. The potnia theron

in Greenland, who used to live largely on seal hunting, "the seals belong to the mistress of animals, Sedna, the Old Woman 'down there.' If a tribe fails to find enough seals, and is threatened with famine, this is a situation for the shaman to step in and help"[20] by negotiating with Sedna. Among the Amazonian Tukano Indians, the *payé,* or shaman, serves as "an intermediary between the hunter and the supernatural 'masters' of the animals. The payé must influence these masters or 'owners' so that they will cede some of their animals" to hunters.[21] The gravity of this reciprocity for indigenous people is illustrated by the Tukano belief that in bargaining with the master of animals, the shaman must promise a certain number of souls of his own people in exchange for the animals killed—and those people after death will morph into animals—but not the hummingbirds the Tukano originate from—to replenish the master's stock.[22]

While the features of the master or mistress of animals fragmented and dispersed as the Greeks moved out of their hunter-gatherer stage, the vital qualities of the potnia theron did not and were taken up by various divine figures of the Grecian pantheon. The "Mistress of Animals was individualized in Greece in various ways, as Hera, Artemis, Aphrodite, Demeter, and Athena."[23] One of her features, that of ensuring fertility cycles, clearly fell to Aphrodite, who in her Homeric hymn is celebrated as "the mother of animals" and is depicted as escorted by dangerous, fawning predators identical to those that unsettled Odysseus's as men.

> And she came to Ida with its many springs, the mother of animals. Behind her moved grey wolves, fawning on her, and bright-eyed lions, bears and quick, insatiable panthers. When she saw them she felt joy in her heart, and she put longing in their breasts, and immediately they all went into the shade of the valley in twos to sleep with each other.[24]

Fig. 5.5. The potnia theron

Much as Circe does, the master or mistress of the animals in other cultures has a dwelling deep in the wild. Among the Tukano Indians he is known as Vaí-mahsë, and "In every ecosystem there exists a 'house' where the Master of Animals dwells. The house may be a rocky hill, a lake, a pool in the river, a large boulder; in any case it will be a permanent feature of the landscape. Such a place is believed to be inhabited by animals and plants invisible to ordinary human beings, but clearly visible to shamans"[25]

Like Circe's mount, "these are sacred places to be avoided, otherwise, Vaí-mahsë will be angered and will punish the offender with illness." Yet these sites have a strong lure: "these dark rocky hills contain what each hunter longs for: animals in abundance, magical plants that give success in the hunt and love."[26]

Among the Innus, offerings can be left at these houses, such as the heaps of "smashed caribou bones" and "piles of caribou antlers, known as windrows, placed in lakes to appease the spirits."[27] Among all cultures, however, these spirit residences are perilous to visit. Just as Odysseus requires the magical plant moly and guidance of Hermes, "Only a hunter in a state of ritual purity, aided by the invocations of a payé [or shaman], dares to go near a hill and obtain these precious gifts with impunity."[28]

It is difficult, then, not to detect the presence of the potnia theron when Odysseus's men, upon first approaching Circe's palace, encounter "mountain wolves and lions roaming round the grounds," who come around them, "fawning, swishing their long tails. As they came nuzzling round—lions, wolves with big powerful claws—the men cringed in fear at the sight of those strange, ferocious beasts" (*Odyssey* 10.231–39).

Such gatherings of marvelous predators belong to the mythic topography of the master or mistress of animals. Below the hilltop dwellings of Vaí-mahsë lie open clearings where huge celebratory dances of animals will take place, which the Tukano know of by the "smell of the many magical plants with which the animals have rubbed their bodies."[29] Sometimes a stray hunter may stumble on an open clearing at the foot of the dwelling of Vaí-mahsë and find the tracks of dancing animals, and "may even find some ornament or perhaps a flute that has been forgotten or lost by the participants of the dance."[30]

During our time in Peru, the jungle spirit Chulla Chacqui, as the master of animals is known in western South America, became familiar. Relaxing after ceremonies, Flores would smoke his *mapacho* of Amazonian tobacco and describe how he had visited the Chulla Chacqui in his visions that evening and how beautiful and fertile his *chacra,* or jungle garden, was. Workers also told us how they had been the butt of jokes or been led astray into the depths of the forest by the mischievous spirit.

Fascinatingly, communication with this master of animals was mediated through his botanical manifestation. Preparations were made of the bark of the stilt-rooted tree, and I witnessed how visitors who drank the potion would be taken on intimate guided tours of the jungle during ceremonies with ayahuasca.

Such "dieting," in which the shaman or patient drinks a preparation of the plant whose spirit he wishes to commune with, leads to profitable communication. Rather like moly for Odysseus, "by following the appropriate diet, it is possible to become the friend of the Chulla Chacqui, which can give hunters luck."[31]

Pablo Amaringo, the visionary bard of Amazonian vegetalismo, painted a jungle scene depicting the residence of the Chulla Chacqui. Wearing a royal gown, surrounded by the denizens of the jungle, the Chulla Chacqui reads a parchment containing a decree on the care of wild animals. According to Amaringo, such a gathering is "like a Bacchanalian feast in which all wild animals are invited. There you can hear the most complex sounds and lullabies of the purity of the forest, of the intimate web of the vegetal esoteric world."[32] Like Aphrodite's and Circe's fawning animals, the beasts are "called through a telepathic vibration in which the instinct of the psychic cord makes the animals come to the meeting."[33]

The clincher in identifying Circe as potnia theron, however, is the shamanic nature of her negotiation with Odysseus, which requires a violent confrontation to release the animals held captive in her realm back into the realm of humanity. One example of this practice, recorded in the seventeenth century, is given among the Eskimos of Greenland, where "a spot in the shaman's tent is marked as if it were a breathing hole of seals in the ice. The shaman conjures Sedna [the mistress of animals] to appear," and, much as Odysseus threatens to run Circe through with his sword, "hits her with his harpoon at the moment she comes up. Triumphantly he shows the blood on his harpoon." Just as Odysseus gains his men's freedom from captivity as animals, in Greenland, as a consequence of the shaman's ambush, "the mistress of animals is forced to set free the seals for a successful hunt."[34]

COURTING THE MISTRESS OF ANIMALS

As we have seen, approaching such a potent divinity as the mistress or master of animals requires shamanic power. In many indigenous cultures, when confronted by a disease or a series of misfortunes—both of which arise from disequilibrium in the spiritual realm—it is normal to resort to spirit/plant allies to diagnose the malady and hunt down a cure. In the Amazon, for example, a shaman will consult plant preparations, creating a threshold state of consciousness in which "the genie of the plant then comes to him in dreams or dreamlike states to cure—and to teach him the secrets about how to empower himself, gain skills and cure."[35]

It is fitting, therefore, that Odysseus sets off to Circe's hall to rescue his men much as the Huichol shaman sets off, with the aid of his peyote-spirit ally Kauyumarie, to rescue the unfortunates trapped within the highly seductive, intoxicating song of the sorcerer Kieri. Sure enough, Odysseus encounters his spirit ally and the plant medicine he requires: "Clambering up through hushed, entrancing glades, as I was nearing the halls of Circe skilled in spells, approaching her palace—Hermes, god of the golden wand, crossed my path, and he looked for all the world like a young man sporting his first beard, just in the prime and warm pride of youth" (*Odyssey* 10.303–8).

It is no coincidence that Hermes, whose staff, the caduceus whose intertwining serpents* may indicate a very early role in the healing arts, manifests next to the very plant medicine required by Odysseus, since such plants act as spiritual antennae, and in threshold states or moments of great need, the resident divinity may manifest in their vicinity.†

Hermes reveals the spiritual origin of Odysseus's misfortune and playfully declares it hopeless, but then states, "But wait, I can save you, free you from that great danger. Look, here is a potent drug. Take it to Circe's halls—its power alone will shield you from the fatal day" (*Odyssey* 10.317–19). He then explains to Odysseus "all the witch's subtle craft," giving him a detailed prescription for breaking Circe's spell. "With that the giant-killer handed over the magic herb, pulling it from the earth, and Hermes showed me all its name and nature," (*Odyssey* 10.335–37) allowing Odysseus to add it to his magical pharmacopeia.

Odysseus gives a description of the moly: "Its root is black and its flower white as milk and the gods call it moly" (*Odyssey* 10.338–39). Full of the sort of respect indigenous cultures demonstrate toward powerful consciousness-altering plants, he states that moly is "dangerous for mortal man to pluck from the soil but not for the deathless gods" (*Odyssey* 10.339–40).

Such reverence for the resident divinities of plants was also demonstrated around the "hunt"[36] for the herbal inebriants of the Dionysian rites. As in

---

*Anthropologist Jeremy Narby writes, "One of the best-known variants of the *axis mundi* is the caduceus, formed by two snakes wrapped around an axis. Since the most ancient times, one finds this symbol connected to the art of healing" (*The Cosmic Serpent,* 95). Given shamanic medicine's need to traverse worlds in order to encounter cures, it is not surprising that the psychopomp and messenger Hermes should be carrying this symbol. A modified version of the caduceus, with only one snake on it, became the staff of the god of medicine, Asclepius, from whom ancient Greek doctors traced their descent.

†They may also show up in unwanted ways. One of us, while "dieting" plant medicines in the deep jungle, was repeatedly awakened in the middle of the night by a tremendous shaking going through our little hut, as if someone were yanking back and forth the poles supporting the structure. It was perplexing, since we weren't in a seismically active region. The next day, Juan Flores pointed out the presence of a large Chulla Chacqui Caspi tree growing right behind the hut, and, laughing, said, "The Chulla Chacqui came and played a trick on you last night!"

Fig. 5.6. Odysseus freeing the encarceled animals

Amazonian vegetalismo, where ayahuasca must be gathered and prepared following observances of "the phase of the moon, the hour of preparation of the beverage, the exclusion of women of fertile age from the place of preparation, the necessity to blow smoke and be constantly present,"[37] the plants used in the Dionysian rites "required magical procedures when gathered."[38] As well, like the ayahuasca vine, which is associated with the jaguar throughout the Amazon, they were similarly viewed as "wild beings whose spirits were akin to their particular guardian animals."[39] Also, considering their power to induce ecstatic rapture, they were "identified as sexual forces."[40]

Indeed, among the Desana of the Colombian Amazon, hunting is an explicitly sexual activity: their verb meaning "to hunt," *vái-merä gametarári,* is translated as "to make love to the animals."[41]

It is no surprise, then, that there is a strong sexual component in Hermes' instructions to Odysseus: "The moment Circe strikes with her long thin wand, you draw your sharp sword sheathed at your hip and rush her fast as if to run her through! She'll cower in fear and coax you to her bed" (*Odyssey* 10.325–28).

This invitation to "mix in the magic work of love" (*Odyssey* 10.371) to the point of rapturous self-mutilation characteristic of the worship of the potnia theron is a dangerous opportunity that Odysseus must navigate to become an intimate of the goddess.* This he does by having her swear an oath that she will not, "once I lie there naked unman me, strip away my courage!" (*Odyssey* 10.378–79)—most likely a euphemism for castration.

Underlying this simple narrative device, we can detect the imprint of generations of accrued experience in encountering the wild forces of the vegetal realm. Plant-induced ecstasy also appears to have been part of the potnia theron's worship as "a goddess whose magic ruled the wild, indeed, for whom all of Being was magical." Her devotees "entered into extreme energetic states in her worship: women tore apart animals in their frenzy, young men at the height of raging sexual ecstasy mutilated themselves in her honor."[42]

Even today, among the peoples of the Amazon, a spirit by the name of Mayita continues to work Circean magic through *pusangas*—love potions. These special preparations of plants, gathered in the jungle while observing the proper diet and sung over with icaros, can draw Mayita to abide in them. As she appeared to doña Maria, a Peruvian curandera, "Mayita is an elegant, beautiful woman, a *perfumera* and *hechicera* (sorceress) and *pusangera*—a caster of spells who creates love potions through the use of perfumes."[43] When doña Maria would sing her icaro, Mayita would come and dance, emitting an especially strong, potent perfume that activated the plant preparation. Often "other spirits may come as well—the yacurunas, the water people, and the sirenas, mermaids, the sexually seductive dwellers beneath the water."[44†]

---

*Not only does moly provide Odysseus with immunity to Circe's brew, it also helps to reveal his closely hidden identity. "You have a mind in *you* no magic can enchant! You must be Odysseus, man of twists and turns," Circe declares upon beholding a man unaffected by her brew. "Hermes the giant killer, god of the golden wand, he always said you'd come" (*Odyssey* 10.365–68). It is only when Odysseus's identity is laid bare that Circe invites him to her bed.

†Indeed, one can wonder about the aphrodisiac effect of the moly plant on Odysseus as well, given the evident phallic symbolism of Hermes' instructions to draw the sword on his hip and rush on Circe as if to "run her through." Male sexual enhancers in the Amazonian pharmacopeia are popularly marketed under labels such as Rompecalzón (Rip Your Shorts), Levántate Lázaro (Arise Lazarus!), and Tumba Hembra (Knock Her Over) (Beyer, *Singing to the Plants,* 194), indicating the Dionysian rush they purport to pack.

Yet Mayita is a garden-variety spirit in comparison to the enchantress Circe, or the even more rapturous power of the Earth goddess Gaia.

To better comprehend the deep imprint of centuries of shamanic experience on the traditions of the ancient Greeks, it is worth considering the myth of Persephone's abduction, for in it we find an identical constellation of plant hunt, resident plant divinity, and communion within the plant divinity's realm as occurs in the *Odyssey*.

In the *Homeric Hymn to Demeter,* wherein is recounted the origin of the rites at Eleusis, we see Persephone, daughter of Demeter, gathering flowers on the Nysian Plain, in a meadow sacred to Dionysus—that seductive abductor of consciousness par excellence. While we do not know their exact species, we do know that the roses, crocuses, violets, irises, and hyacinths the maiden was gathering were considered psychoactive drugs by the ancients. Persephone, that fact alone suggests, is not an innocent lass gathering a bouquet.

A trap, or initiation, has been set for the maiden by the Earth mother Gaia, baited by a plant of great otherworldly potency—the narcissus, "a flower wondrous and bright, awesome for all to see, for the immortals above and for mortals below. From its root a hundredfold bloom sprang up and smelled so sweet that the whole vast heaven above and the whole earth laughed, and the salty swell of the sea" (10–14).[45] Such description overleaps the botanical to evoke the pure realm, the psychoactive properties, that even its scent exudes.

Persephone reaches to pluck the narcissus, whose heavily weighted blossoms disguise the fact that in them lies death: Hades and his horses lurk within its molecular radiance, waiting to break apart the veil between the worlds and abduct Persephone into his realm. Like moly, through whom the spirit of Hermes manifests, in the narcissus we can see that "the spirit that inhabits a magic plant might also be something else: an empirical entity that addresses a person who ingests the plant."[46]

As the tale goes, Hades abducts the maiden. Persephone utterly vanishes, leaving behind only an echoing cry. Her mother, Demeter, eventually aided by Hekate and Helios, begins a search for her daughter and uncovers the truth of her abduction. In the face of Zeus's inaction, Demeter vanishes from the sight of the Olympians, and as goddess of the harvest and seasons, renders the fields infertile, and famine stalks the Earth. Disguised as an old crone, she arrives in the city of Eleusis and is received as a nurse into the royal household. There she sets in motion the founding of the Eleusinian mysteries that her daughter will bring to fruition. In the meantime, Zeus capitulates and sends Hermes to fetch Persephone back. Famously, before departing, Persephone eats a pomegranate seed or two, which she is slipped by Hades, binding her to the underworld. Following the mother and daughter's tearful reunion, it emerges that her daughter must now "spend one-third of the revolving year in the misty dark, and two-thirds with her mother and the other immortals" (463–65). Demeter reconciles herself to sharing her daughter and goes to the leaders of Eleusis and

> . . . *taught her Mysteries to all of them,*
> *holy rites that are not to be transgressed, nor pried into,*
> *nor divulged. For a great awe of the gods stops the voice.*
> *Blessed is the mortal on earth who has seen these rites,*
> *but the uninitiated who has no share in them never*
> *has the same lot once dead in the dreary darkness.* (476–82)

In approaching this ancient tale, it is worth recalling the oral tradition's technique of transmitting information through "lively, dynamic, often violent, characters and encounters."[47] Setting aside our horror of and repugnance for the act of abduction and rape, we can ask what the message of the hymn is in using such a violent, dynamic motif.

We may be doing Persephone's myth an injustice by characterizing her solely as a naïve maiden, a pawn in the marriage brokerage business of Zeus, conducted without her mother Demeter's consent.

While Persephone may be first seen in the *Hymn* as an innocent, reaching for the narcissus as a "lovely toy" (16), the narrative points toward an initiatory ordeal. If Persephone is a pharmakeus in her own right, it is natural that she, like Odysseus, hunts for plants with magical properties and turns out to be equally responsive to the resident divinities within them. Persephone's lineage also suggests her status as a pharmakeus: according to classicist Karl Kerenyi, Demeter probably "brought the poppy with her from her Cretan cult to Eleusis."[48] As is traditional in such accounts, Persephone is only named once prior to her marriage to Hades: before she is simply Korē, the maiden or daughter. "Because initiates often receive adult names in the course of initiation rituals into adulthood . . . the poem may be marking a change of identity or Korē's acquisition of new powers as goddess of the underworld."[49]

The initiatory, sexual nature of this initiatory abduction is suggested by the etymological detective work of classicist Carl Ruck, who thinks that abduction "is code for both pharmacological ecstasy and the holy marriage (hierosgamos) of a maiden to the god of death in the form of the spirit who 'is' the true identity of the magic plant."[50] In other words, the ego death through ravishment into a plant divinity's realm is also a marriage with that spirit.

In light of the mysteries founded upon her induction into the realm of the dead, we could also read Persephone as *choosing* her ordeal of abduction, as does Odysseus in approaching Circe's seat or undergoing his ordeal of listening to the Siren's song.

As we shall see in detail later, the shaman's work is to navigate this abduction of self within the plant realm, as Odysseus does in his battle to win Circe as an ally, to bridge the human and divine. Through interlacing the wild plant's divinity in her or his own body, the shaman grows to abide in multiple realms. In the myth of Persephone's abduction, we see this process on a cosmological level in her transformation into the great liberator of human souls from the prison house of Hades through the rites of the Eleusinian mysteries.

We know very little about the actual content of these sacred rites, which endured for two thousand years, but we are given glimpses into the initiatory experience itself by ancient authors, such as when Plutarch, drawing on the experience of the mysteries, describes the soul at the moment of death.

> The soul suffers an experience similar to those who celebrate great initiations. . . . Wandering astray in the beginning, tiresome walkings in circles, some frightening paths in darkness that lead nowhere; then immediately before the end all the terrible things, panic and shiver-

ing and sweat, and amazement. And then some wonderful light comes to meet you, pure regions and meadows are there to greet you, with sounds and dances and solemn, sacred words and holy views, and there the initiate, perfect by now, set free and loose from all bondage, walks about, crowned with a wreath, celebrating the festival together with the other sacred, and pure people, and he looks down on the uniniti-ated, unpurified crowd in this world in mud and fog beneath his feet.[51]

As Aristotle emphasized, "The initiate does not learn [*mathein*] something but is made to experience [*pathein*] the Mysteries and change his or her state of mind."[52] Indeed, so potent were the blessings of these initiatory experiences, the garments of initiates "were later used as swad-dling clothes for newborn babies."[53]

As in the grand cosmological sweep of the Eleusinian mysteries, so in the humble vegetalista tradition of the Amazon, plant divinities fulfill the role of bridging the realms of life and death. As Juan Flores explained to us, "Ayahuasca helps us to die, because when we die, we encounter strong spirits. In ceremonies we may die and be reborn many times—we live, we die, we live, we die. So we have the opportunity to learn how to die with ayahusaca, to know death very closely."[54]

To conclude this far-ranging excursion through the indigenous experi-ence of plant sentience: wily Odysseus receives the chthonic plant moly, whose power allows him to clearly perceive and negotiate with the god-dess Circe. Entering the dwelling of the mistress of animals, Odysseus follows the instructions of the plant/spirit ally to the letter and passes his initiatory ordeal, freeing his men from animal captivity. Yet despite his seduction of Circe and his sojourn in her restorative realm, his travails are not over. As we have seen in the case of Persephone, his path is to be a downward-spiraling one.

Circe is going to send Odysseus to the land of the dead.

SIX

ANIMAL *BECOMING*

We can understand, too, that natural species are chosen not because they are "good to eat" but because they are "good to think."

CLAUDE LEVI-STRAUSS

Is this account below, published in 1705 in Virginia, a colonial version of Odysseus's crew members' strange adventure in Circe's palace?

This being an early plant, was gather'd by some Soldiers sent thither, and some of them eat plentifully of it, the Effect of which was a very pleasant Comedy; for they turn'd natural Fools upon it for several Days; One would blow up a Feather in the air; another would dart straws at it with much Fury; and another stark naked was sitting up in a corner, like a Monkey, grinning and making Mows at them; a Fourth would fondly kiss, and paw his Companions, and snear in their Faces, with a Countenance more antick, than any in a *Dutch* Droll. In this frantick Condition they were confined, lest they should in their Folly destroy themselves; though it was observed, that all their Actions were full of Innocence and good Nature A Thousand such simple tricks they play'd, and after Eleven Days, return'd to themselves again, not remembering any thing that had pass'd.[1]

90

Or perhaps it is an interlude among the Lotus Eaters, about which Homer relates, "Any crewman who ate the lotus, the honey-sweet fruit, lost all desire to send a message back, much less return, their only wish to linger there with the Lotus Eaters, grazing on lotus, all memory of the journey home dissolved forever"? (*Odyssey* 9.106–10).

In fact, it is a historical record of what happened to the English soldiers who ate of the species *Datura stramonium,* back then known as "Jamestown weed," now shortened to jimsonweed. The soldiers' ingestion of this powerful narcotic may not have been accidental—the soldiers may have learned about the plant from the original inhabitants of Virginia, who used it in their initiation rites.

The uncanny similarity between the experiences of Odysseus's men and the English soldiers may arise from the fact that, as a pharmakeus, or expert concoctor of potions, Circe mixes not just opium into the wine, but a member of the Solanaceae family, which includes the famous narcotic plants of medieval witchcraft: mandrake, henbane, deadly nightshade, and datura. These plants, which "have played a role in religion, magic, divination, sorcery, and medicine in different parts of the world since ancient times,"[2] can create a temporary loss of memory and near-complete suggestibility.* At high doses, these plants, also held sacred by many indigenous peoples, can cause transformations into animals or facilitate a death-rebirth initiatory ordeal.†

The motif of initiatory rebirth in the narcotic womb is a recurrent theme in the ancient world, where it was often symbolized as a cauldron. On the silver Gundestrup Cauldron found in Denmark, dating from the

---

*According to anthropologist Jeremy Narby, a current practice of this ancient method is found among urban criminals in Colombia. It is called *burundanga:* "Datura extracts are sprayed on people and they become willing victims. People are told to go home and get their money, get their jewelry, bring them back and give them to the person, go down to the bank, empty their bank accounts, and then these people end up 3 or 4 hours later, dazed and confused, they get taken to a hospital and their blood is tested and they find scopolamine in it" (Narby, "Interview Jeremy Narby, part 3 of 4").

†One of the most important types of alkaloid found in the Solanaceae family is tropane, whose name comes from the belladonna genus *Atropa,* appropriately named after the Greek Fate Atropos, the one who cuts the thread of life.

Fig. 6.1. The cauldron of rebirth

first century BCE, we see a procession of warriors trudging toward a giant figure who dunks them headfirst into a vat, after which they ride away on horses, evidently the better for the experience.

A similar magical cauldron, also with the power to restore the dead to life after immersion in its dark interior, appears in the Second Branch of the medieval Welsh *Mabinogi*. The underlying symbolic connection between these Northern myths and that of Circe is illustrated by the inclusion of a cauldron in a "Homeric scene enacted on a Greek black-figure vase depicting Circe and Odysseus in which the shaman/sorceress uses her transformational cauldron to change the Hero's followers into pigs."[3]

Once again, Native American shamanic tradition offers an illuminating perspective on the fantastical experiences that take place in the halls of Circe.

The Indians of Virginia used *Datura* in boys' initiation rites—rites that display the death-rebirth theme of rites of passage characteristic of all such ordeals.

"When the time for initiation had been set for the elders, the young men and boys were taken into the forest, where they were kept in strict seclusion in a specially constructed hut of latticework"[4] (à la Circe's pens!). There they were given *Datura,* after which they "became stark, staring mad, in which raving condition they were kept eighteen or twenty days."[5] Akin to Circe's beneficially healthful transformation of Odysseus's crewmen into swine, who, when she restores them by "anointing them one by one with some new magic oil," are "younger than ever, taller by far, more handsome to the eye" (*Odyssey* 10.433–37), the Virginia Indians would emerge having, according to colonial historian Robert Beverley's 1705 account, "unlived their former lives, and commence Men, by forgetting that they have ever been Boys. . . . They hope by this proceeding, to root out all the prepossessions and unreasonable prejudices which are fixt in the minds of Children. So that, when the Young men come to themselves again, their Reason may act freely . . . establish't in a state of equality and perfect freedom."[6]

Indigenous peoples with continuous cultural traditions still recognize the rejuvenating power of immersion in plant consciousness. Bob Boyll, who trained among the Huichol, related to me the account of an old Huichol mentor of his, who, well past his hundredth year, took a turn for the worse. His family conducted a series of peyote ceremonies for him, at the end of which not only had he recuperated, but his white hair was visibly growing out black again from the roots!*

Not all such transformations are benevolent, however. Anthropologist Peter Furst gives an account of a punishment meted out to an individual held responsible for the betrayal and death of a popular peasant leader in Mexico some years ago. This "wretched man was turned over to a local bruja—a word meaning 'witch,'" who, "by judicious combination of repeated infusions of *Datura* and a play on his guilt feelings, together with hypnotic suggestion, brought the man to a state where for several months, until his death, he walked, barked, fed, and was treated like a dog—a fate some of the local people seemed to think he deserved only too well."[7]

It is likely that the Virginia Indians experienced transformation into animals while entranced, since, as we will see, such capacity appears neurologically hardwired into the human species. It is certain that during the

---

*Such vitalizing effects may also be seen in Tolkien's account of the ent-draught that Fangorn, or Treebeard, gives to Merry and Pippin, who not only increased in stature after drinking it, but could feel "the hair on their heads was actually standing up, waving and curling and growing" (Tolkien 2004, p. 471).

Datura initiations of the Luiseño Indians of California interspecies communication occurred. This experience "became of lifelong intimate sanctity to them. This vision is usually of an animal, and at least at times they learn from it a song which they keep as their own. It is certain a special and individual relation of a supernatural kind is believed to exist forever after between the dreamer and the dream."[8]

If the archaeological record is to be believed, the oldest game in town, after procreation, is animal transformation. Following the delicious mammoth bone figurines of the Paleolithic Venuses, whose generous, open vulvas and swollen breasts bespeak fecundity and nourishment, the oldest surviving images of prehistoric Europe are representations of animal *becoming.* The earliest yet found, a portable statuette of a human body and feline head from a cave in Hohlenstein-Stadel, Germany, has astonishing time depth: dating to 32,000 BCE.

Subsequent art, such as the *therianthrops,* or sorcerers, of the painted caves of France, shows the long trajectory of these representations—these

Fig. 6.2. The Hohlenstein-Stadel lion man

famous animal-human dancing figures of Les Trois-Frères cave were painted a full twenty thousand years *after* the carving of the Hohlenstein-Stadel lion man.

These mysterious traces of human–animal symbiosis resurface in the earliest literature of the West. As we have seen, story in the ancient world, while delighting in the fantastical, was never just that. In oral culture, these accounts were faithfully transmitted from generation to generation to entertain, instruct, and preserve ancestral memory and practices. Such literature survives as a hoary remnant of our ancient symbiosis with animals, which, alien as it may seem today, was almost certainly among the earliest conscious experiences of our species. In this way, works such as the *Odyssey,* the Norse *Saga of the Volsungs,* and the Celtic *Mabinogi* exhibit kinship with this mysterious cave art.

Repositories of far more ancient folklore and spiritual practice than the date of their actual composition, these written works contain numerous accounts of animal *becoming.*

In the *Saga of the Volsungs,* Sigmund and Sinfjotli, surviving as guerrilla fighters in the wilderness of Gautland, find a house, inside of which are two sleeping men with thick gold rings, on whom a spell has been cast. Above them hang wolfskins that they can only shed every tenth day.

> Sigmund and Sinfjotli put the skins on and could not get them off. And the weird power was there as before: they howled like wolves, both understanding the sounds. Now, they set out into the forest, each going his own way. They agreed that they would risk a fight with as many as seven men, but not more, and that the one being attacked by more would howl with his wolf's voice.[9]

Rather like Sigmund and Sinfjotli, the Berserkers, who also appear in the Icelandic sagas, were traditionally associated with the spirit of the bear and were renowned for their battle frenzy. Wearing nothing but bear pelts, according to Snorri Sturluson in the *Ynglinga Saga,* men rushed forwards without armor, were as mad as dogs or wolves, bit their shields, and were strong as bears or wild bulls, and killed people at a blow, but neither fire nor iron told upon them. This was called *Berserk-gang.*[10]

In the Celtic *Mabinogi,* we find animal *becoming* inflicted as a punishment in a manner reminiscent of the one meted out to the betrayer of the peasant leader in Mexico. In this medieval Welsh text, the magician Gwydion and his brother, Gilfaethwy, found guilty of the rape of a maiden, are struck by King Math's staff of enchantment and are transformed into beasts, in this case, a good-size hind and stag. "Since you two are inseparable," says Math, "I will make you travel together and mate in the same manner as the wild beasts in whose shape you are; and when they have offspring, so shall you. A year from today, return here to me.

"Let your nature be the same as that of the animals in whose shape you are,"[11] adds Math, yet there the nature of the punishment implies that Gwydion and Gilfaethwy also retain human consciousness, much as in the *Odyssey,* where Odysseus's men kept "their minds steadfast as before" (*Odyssey* 10.265). It is worth noting that ancient Greek depictions of Odysseus's crew show them as the prehistoric lion man of Hohlenstein-Stadel, with human bodies and animal heads, rather than as entire swine, perhaps indicating symbiosis between animal and human consciousness, rather than total metamorphosis.

A year hence, a stag and hind appear, accompanied by a sturdy fawn. Math adopts their offspring, turning the fawn into a human, and sends Gwydion and Gilfaethwy off in the form of a sow and boar. After another year, the cycle is repeated again, and they are sent off as a wolf and bitch. Three animal–human creatures come from these matings, about whom Math, upon restoring their final offspring to human form, chants:

> *Three sons of wicked Gilfaethwy,*
> *Three true champions*
> *Bleiddwn, Hyddwn and Hychdwn Hir.*[12]

Given the nature of ancient initiations, it is likely that these supernaturally conceived youth are offspring of rites involving animal transformation.

That animal transformation is among the most significant of shamanic experiences is testified to not only by its astonishing time depth in Europe, but also by its wide distribution throughout the Americas.

Intensified encounters with the New World feline, the jaguar, held a crucial role in the cosmology of the ancient civilizations, as well as the surviving present-day tribes of South America. So deep was the symbiosis that one is given the impression that human and jaguar consciousnesses were inextricably interwoven at the origin of human emergence.

For example, among the Kogis, "the myths tell of huge, ferocious jaguars that, at the beginning of time, were born of the Universal Mother, and of the Jaguar People, who were the descendants of this mythical race and at the same time the direct ancestors of the modern Kogis."[13] The earliest culture heroes as well emerge from jaguar–human unions. In Paez mythology, "a young Indian woman was raped by a jaguar, and from this union the Thunder-Jaguar was born. The child grew into a man, who became an important cultural hero."[14]

In the practice of shamanism, "the close association between shamanism and jaguar–spirits is a widespread complex in American aboriginal cultures. Stated briefly, the basic idea is that the shaman can turn into a jaguar at will, using the form of this animal in disguise, sometimes in order to achieve beneficial ends, sometimes to threaten or to kill."[15] Among the Parakanã, "dreams about jaguars are always associated with metamorphosis, and sometimes are directly connected to a jaguar killing. Some dreamers are capable of 'bringing in' a real jaguar during their oneiric experience and, subsequently, of transforming themselves into one. Such metamorphosis is termed *jyromonem,* which literally means, 'to put a continent on,' that is, 'to dress.' The dreamer brings the jaguar and enters its skin, and, endowed with all its abilities, he goes into the forest to hunt and eat."[16]

Such traditions are found not merely in the reports of anthropologists studying extinct cultures, either. Among the Juaroni people today, the elders still withdraw into the forest to die so as not to endanger their communities when they metamorphose into jaguars.

Shamans, of course, can also bring in a jaguar by directing the visions of those under their sphere of influence, as the Peruvian vegetalista Manuel Córdova-Rios narrated in his description of leading an ayahuasca ceremony with a group of men of Chuzúta.

> With evocative songs, imitated jungle sounds, and subtle gestures creating an atmosphere suitable for auto-suggestion I brought into our joint visions scenes of the forest, where birds of brilliant plumage and rare song were followed by game birds, then by the hunters—the hawks and the owls. . . . A snake-eating hawk doing battle with a fer-de-lance or yellow beard then started a procession of snakes through their visions . . . to impress them I brought into our visions the shuffling, giant, big-headed spotted cat of old Chief Xumu's visions. Now as we watched him in wonder, this huge cat stumbled through the trees, grunting to himself, his tongue lolling out, his great curved fangs clearly visible. He looked harmless enough in spite of his size, until with a sudden lashing switch of his tail he became instantly and viciously alert—flashing eyes and a menacing growl. From my seated companions came a collective audible response, a gasp of indrawn death, in anticipation of disaster. But the mighty beast of our fantasy faded from the visioned forest . . .[17]

This ancient symbiosis of animal-human consciousness underlying the hunt still lies latent within the modern psyche. Bob Boyll related how, upon a visit to Eastern Europe to help in peyote ceremonies and sweat lodges, the participants requested a deer dance from him. After leading them through the ceremonial steps he had practiced with his Huichol elders years before, "To my amazement," related Boyll, "a small herd of European red deer stepped out of the woods surrounding the field, and, led by a stag, approached the circle of dancers." The sound of their hooves then joined the pattern being made by the human feet, and for a time the humans and the deer danced together, unified. The stag then stood forth and came right up to the circle and appeared to stomp once in salutation to the humans. The herd then immediately wheeled about and returned to the woods.

"That was medicine in the old ways," Boyll said.

Animal *becoming* can lead to some startling juxtapositions, such as one recorded in the mid-1500s when a German seafarer, Hans Staden, encountered a Tupinambá chief eating a human leg out of a "great vessel full of human flesh." Holding the limb to Staden's mouth, the chief invited him to try it. Staden replied, "Even beasts which were without understanding did not eat their own species, and should a man devour his fellow creatures?" At that, the chief took a bite and turning Staden's argument on its head, replied, "I am a tiger; it tastes well."[18]

Such accounts serve, as anthropologist Carlo Fausto reminds us, that not all shamanism is "loving animism." Indeed, sometimes, "it is better understood as a predatory animism."[19]

This human–feline symbiosis did not just find expression among Amazonian tribes. In Mesoamerican culture, "even on the level of elaborately structured belief systems and an institutionalized priesthood, the jaguar plays an important role. . . . From this association the concept of the were-jaguar, or *nahual,* has arisen, the feline monster with supernatural powers or, in reverse, the shaman with feline attributes."[20]

The most impressive remains of a civilization immersed in feline consciousness is found in Las Mesitas, a sacred complex, no doubt like Stonehenge serving as a ceremonial center for a widely distributed population, located above San Agustín, Colombia. There, among the truly massive, carved monoliths also reminiscent of the menhirs of old Europe, the jaguar is the primary motif.

The civilization of San Agustín, which flourished during the first millennium CE and had already declined and vanished before the arrival of the Spaniards, left behind a phantasmagoric iconography whose symbolism is "rooted in the forests of the Amazon": fanged eagles, toads emerging from boulders, men metamorphosing into cats, snakes from whose tails emerge faces, felines overpowering women or copulating with men, jaguar-toothed rodents; all retain, according to ethnobotanist Wade Davis, "a brooding ferocity, a taut, aggressive power that seems at every moment ready to burst out of the confines of the stone."[21] But, as anthropologist Gerardo Reichel-Dolmatoff stated, "There can be no doubt that this iconographic motif of a man turned into a ferocious feline creature is predominant and that it has a remarkable continuity in time, having persisted for centuries and perhaps millennia."[22]

These statues, with their "heavily compressed human body with an enormous head whose composite features—bared fangs, glaring eyes, and flaring nostrils—represent a snarling feline" and whose "posture expresses the crouching, menacing force contained in this being,"[23] clearly express huma–feline symbiosis.

Fig. 6.3. San Agustín jaguar man

They also express animal *becoming,* which is underscored by the fact that "it was obviously the sculptor's intention not so much to make a jaguar into a man as the reverse. . . . The body, no matter how distorted or compressed, is essentially human; the arms terminate in fingers, not claws, and the legs, however shortened, are human legs. Even eyes and ears are humanoid, although the former vary widely in shape and often have a catlike slant. The short, stubby nose, with its flaring nostrils, although quite out of proportion, is more human than animal . . . by their very exaggeration they blend easily with the bestial mouth into a dreadful, nonhuman face."[24]

Plant consciousness evidently played a key role in the creation of this iconography, called the "earliest evidence of [coca's] sacred role in the lost civilizations of the northern Andes."[25] Davis, gazing on one of the imposing columnar guardian statues over whose head "loomed a spirit being, protective and domineering," noted that, "in each of the cheeks" of the warrior figure "was a prominent bulge. . . . There was no mistaking the resemblance of the stone cheeks to the face of a modern *coquero*."[26]

THE INTENSIFIED TRAJECTORY OF CONSCIOUSNESS

It has long been argued that such transformations were facilitated by ingestion of psychoactive plants. As early as 1784, a Swedish professor named Samuel Ödman shrewdly suggested that the *Amanita muscaria* mushroom was responsible for the Berserkers' fury. Far less frequently considered is the possibility that the nature of such shamanic states is not pathological. Indeed, as in the case of Odysseus's men, who emerge from animal *becoming* "younger than ever, taller by far, more handsome to the eye," the wild infusion of animal vitality and wisdom can even be key to healing trauma and restoring a healthful, balanced homeostasis to the mind and body.

Cognitive archaeologist and anthropologist David Lewis-Williams claims that such a transmutative, potentiating capacity is hardwired in our nervous system, and in his work *The Mind in the Cave* offers a neurophysiological model for the process of entering that "mental vortex that leads to the experiences and hallucinations of deep trance," an entry he claims was psychologically indistinguishable for Upper Paleolithic people from their actual entrance into "the subterranean passages and chambers . . . the 'entrails' of the nether world" of the prehistoric painted caves.[27]

In other words, the ritual activity of entering the caves for early people mirrored the psychophysical experience of entering trance, a biological inheritance of the human species.

What, then, is this hardwiring we all share? According to Lewis-Williams, the ordinary spectrum of consciousness of *Homo sapiens* ranges from a waking, problem-solving orientation to dream and beyond the edge of the psychic world, unconsciousness, as expressed graphically in figure 6.4, shown on the next page.

As we can see from Lewis-Williams's schema, when shamanically intensified, consciousness takes a different fork in the road before entering the realm of hypnagogia. Rather than counting sheep or seeing dancing sugarplums, we begin to perceive "entoptic phenomena," that is, geometrical will-o'-the-wisps that begin to dance before our eyes and "flicker, scintillate, expand, contract, and combine"[28] to draw us on, just as the "embellishing images" of the prehistoric caves "blazed a path into the unknown."[29]

In the second stage of this intensified trajectory, rather than entering the dream state, "Subjects try to make sense of entoptic phenomena by elaborating them into iconic forms."[30] A struggle to focus occurs, and "the brain attempts to decode these forms as it does impressions supplied by the nervous system in an alert, outwardly-directed state."[31] This stage of construal is normally rather brief, a final preparatory moment before the leap into what Lewis-Williams terms "hallucinations."

Lewis-Williams may be mischaracterizing the nature of the third stage, however. The word *hallucination,* whose Latin root, *hallucinari,* means "to wander the mind," no longer carries its ancient signification. The ancient philosopher Heraclitus, speaking of wandering the depths of the mind, or what we now call the "unconscious," could state, "You could not find the ends of the soul though you traveled every way, so deep is its logos."[32] Sadly, modern culture is far more suspicious of those depths, even labeling them with the dismissive term *Id* ("the It.") "To wander the mind," to hallucinate, now means to be mistaken, deluded, or mad. I would, therefore, suggest the more neutral term *visionary* for the experience of this stage.

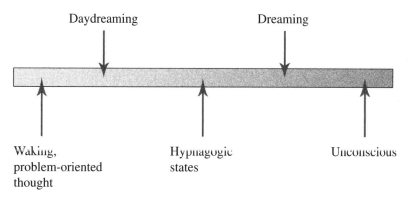

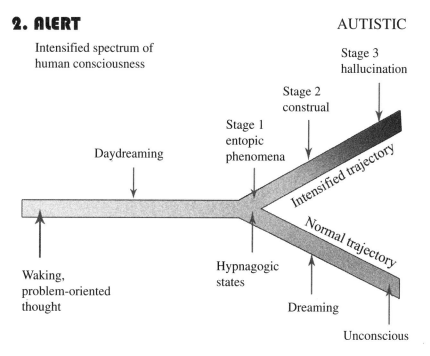

The two spectra of consciousness: (1) "normal consciousness" that drifts from alert to somnolent states, and (2) the "intensified trajectory" that leads to hallucinations

Fig. 6.4. Lewis-Williams's intensified trajectory of consciousness

According to Lewis-Williams, much like passing through the birth canal, in this third stage "many people experience a whirling vortex or rotating tunnel that seems to surround them and draw them into its depths."[33] Often a "bright light in the centre of the field of vision creates this tunnel-like perspective,"[34] and then they are drawn into full interaction with the powers of worlds that lie beyond our ordinary consciousness.

All of this should sound strangely familiar. Alice's drowsy encounter with the White Rabbit and subsequent fall down the rabbit hole into Wonderland might come to mind, or the Pevensie siblings' entrance through the wardrobe into Narnia, or Neo's rebirth experience after taking the red pill in the film *The Matrix*.

The virtue of Lewis-Williams's model is its elegant simplicity. Yet he may be making too much of neurological hardwiring, offering as it does an objective-sounding mechanistic model for transformations of consciousness. Those who have experience with shamanic practices find the idea that consciousness can be reduced to the brain's hardwiring naively solipsistic, and point to not-infrequent episodes in which objective, verifiable information is obtained in visionary states, not to mention a number of other common experiences whose origins defy reduction to the gray matter of the brain.

Lewis-Williams's theory is also a rough fit. For example, the vortex and its ancillary, shamanic flight, which he makes much of, are not that widely reported by contemporary shamans or their Western apprentices (unless, as we shall see below, such flight is accompanied by a specific raptor or another avian medicine). Emphasis on these features appears to be a holdover from Mircea Eliade's early studies of shamanism, focusing on the peoples of the Siberian tundra.

The native voice of a Huichol shaman gives a better idea of this leap into the visionary stage: there is a doorway within our minds that usually remains hidden and secret until the time of death. The Huichol word for it is *nieríka*. *Nieríka* is a cosmic portal or interface between so-called ordinary and nonordinary realities. It is a passageway and at the same time a barrier between worlds.[35]

Among the Tukano, this cosmic portal is encountered when "the payé enters into the state of *ventúri,* of hallucination, which takes him to the blue zone where he meets Vihó-mahsë." Vihó-mahsë is an amoral entity from whom the payé can solicit "good or evil: he can kill persons by sending an illness to them, or he can cure them of their afflictions."[36] It is through Vihó-mahsë that the payé can be transported to the Milky Way and can "view the Milky Way as a road, the hills and pools as malocas, and the animals as persons."*[37]

What is certain is that a threshold is crossed, one that can be subtle or dramatic, where consciousness floats free of the gravitational pull of what Lewis-Williams calls "the problem-solving mind" and reestablishes itself, after a brief stage of construal, in an expanded, visionary state.

Such microscoping or telescoping of consciousness, for the purpose of uncovering hidden layers of reality, is also familiar in the history of science. The chemist August Kekulé, frustrated in his quest for the structure of the benzene molecule, fell asleep in front of a fire and dreamt of an atomic dance (entoptic and construal), out of which arose a molecular snake with its tail in its mouth (visionary). This sign he correctly interpreted as the closed carbon-ring structure of the molecule, and was eventually to recommend to his fellow scientists, "Let us learn to dream, gentlemen."[38]

In a more recent, deliberate experimental attempt to use the intensified visionary state for scientific research, identification with a "protein" was reported by a molecular scientist who drank ayahuasca with Juan Flores. The researcher, who normally worked on deciphering the human genome, "saw a chromosome from the perspective of a protein flying above a long strand of DNA. Seeing the 'CpG islands,' which she had been puzzling over at work . . . she saw they were structurally different

---

*An additional fork may need to be added to Lewis-Williams's map of the intensified trajectory—an upper road into visionary states and a lower one into psychosis. The Tukano also report that those who do not have "the ability to see visions" on hallucinogens "see only clouds and stones, and 'the birds laugh at them.'" In their trance they tear off their loincloths and walk around naked, without shame; they even urinate or defecate in public. But others, the truly experienced payés, control these impulses" (Reichel-Dolmatoff, *Amazonian Cosmos,* 130).

from the surrounding DNA and that this structural difference allowed them to be easily accessed and therefore to serve as 'landing pads' for transcription proteins."[39]

Such dreaming again reminds us of the meaning of *seeing* in the shamanic and ancient worlds. "In Greek as well as Latin—when the verb occurs in an emotionally charged context—[it] always means more than just 'to observe' or 'to witness' something; it means 'to experience,' 'to be involved in a meaningful event.'"[40]

It also reminds us that the "especially vivid" vision in the intensified trajectory, where "transcosmological travel and preternatural sight go hand in hand,"[41] can help guide us in our tangible lives.

Such was the experience of my friend Anders, a Swedish pilot and wing-walking stuntman who first *saw* the land his family now runs an animal sanctuary on during a flyover. At the time he was penniless and not hunting for land, but the certainty that he was *seeing* his future home was electric.

In a subsequent, unannounced flyover with his wife, Montrese, she also *saw* it: "As we flew directly over it, I felt a surge of energy in my solar plexus. I looked down and saw a plateau of golden pastoral beauty that fit our dreams perfectly. I put my hand on his shoulder and said into his ear over the loud noise of the airplane's engine, 'That's it! That's it!' He nodded and said, 'I know.' When we landed we compared notes on how we had each been drawn to this one piece of land out in the middle of nowhere."

Eventually the land was offered to them for sale—again, out of the blue.

It was therefore in character that, upon participating in a peyote ceremony on his land, Anders found himself metamorphosing into an eagle and sailing over the landscape he loves so much. "But the exactness of the detail," he told me, shaking his head in wonder, "the complete specificity. I really was flying and *seeing* all these places. I would travel into town and visit areas I was curious about, getting a clear sense of the features and topography of the land.

"I also hate snakes," he added. "I mean, I really loathe reptiles and have never been able to overcome that revulsion. So it came as a real surprise when I found myself hungry for one. I was returning from a long flight and found myself fantasizing about finding a nice snake for dinner!"*

That evening, as Anders sailed far from his body's physical locale in the tipi, a Diné elder was making his way around the circle. Anders was suddenly recalled to his body to find the man gazing into his face, as if searching a distant landscape.

"I've only been looked at like that a few times in my life," Anders said.

After the ceremony the elder came up to the couple and gave Anders a gift: an eagle feather.

"It will take care of you," the Navajo assured him.

"It was like a crack of thunder," Montrese told me, "because I was the only one who knew all the Eagle medicine that Anders had been undergoing."

Having passed through the mental vortex of the intensified trajectory, the subject becomes "part of a strange realm," where "people sometimes feel themselves to be turning into animals and undergoing other frightening or exalting transformations."[42]

Upon immersion into the fathomless depths of the third stage, the

---

*The empirical, objective quality of some of the data derived from animal *becoming* has been recorded by researcher Stan Grof in patients' sessions with LSD during the 1950s and later using the method of holotropic breathwork, in which, he said, "transpersonal experience involves a complete and realistic identification with members of various animal species" (Grof, *The Adventure of Self Discovery*, 52–53), including even cephalopods (octopus and squid) and gastropods (snails and slugs)! As in the case of the usage of altered states by indigenous hunters to study the behavior of their prey, Westerners can "gain experiential insight into what it feels like when a cat is curious, an eagle frightened, a cobra hungry, a turtle sexually aroused, or when a shark is breathing through the gills" (Grof, *The Adventure of Self Discovery*, 52–53). Accompanying the transformation is a "sense of time regression and the feeling that the individual is exploring the evolutionary lines of phylogenetic development" (Grof, *LSD: Doorway to the Numinous*, 183–84).

There is a clearly heuristic value to these visions. Verifiable, experiential insights into such phenomena as the vision of raptor birds or the fat storage mechanism of a lioness do occur.

subject experiences a profoundly meaningful participation in the vast, strange, and intensely beautiful sentience of the cosmos, as Odysseus does in Hades or as the Tukano tribe of the Colombian Amazon does in their aya-huasca ceremonies, where "they see yajé snakes, the Master of the Animals who withholds animals or releases them to hunters, the Sun-Father, the Daughter of the Anaconda, and other mythical beings."[43]

While Lewis-Williams's cognitive archaeology and anthropology provide a good, workable model for how indigenous peoples and the ancient Greeks could "take hold of the possibilities of the intensified trajectory" and "harness the human brain,"[44] it is necessary to part company with him in his interpretation of the workings of the intensified state, for Lewis-Williams claims that ultimately not only shamanic experience, but even dream states are mere exhaust fumes of brain activity. As vestiges of our slow evolution into rationality, visionary experience, much less indigenous perception of a sentient, vital cosmos, have no intrinsic value to waking consciousness for Lewis-Williams.

Other anthropologists and ethnobotanists, of course, have been more open to the inherent worth of indigenous experience and the visionary stage of the intensified trajectory. Richard Evans Schultes, for example, didn't hesitate to dance with and immerse himself in the practices of his native hosts, and so came to know the power of the plants of his beloved Amazonian peoples from within.

Yet one of the greatest explorers of the intensified trajectory of consciousness, arguably the foremost in restoring the prestige of primal consciousness to the modern world, never visited the Amazon, danced with indigenous tribes, or drank consciousness-altering potions.

SEVEN

J. R. R. TOLKIEN AND THE INTENSIFIED TRAJECTORY OF CONSCIOUSNESS

Have you believed in jaguars? Have you believed that,
when dying, you will turn into a jaguar?

EIGHTEENTH-CENTURY INTERROGATORY
OF FRANCISCAN FRIARS USED IN CONFESSING
THE SIONA INDIANS OF THE SOUTHERN COLOMBIAN AMAZON

Although Middle Earth could easily be characterized as a product of the intensified trajectory, J. R. R. Tolkien, staunch Catholic, Oxford don, one of the most brilliant philologists of his age, gives scant evidence of a shaman adventurer. "I am in fact a hobbit,"[1] he once wrote, describing his conservative and simple tastes.

Like Bilbo, he preferred to hear the singing of his kettle as he puttered around in his garden, leading his biographer, Humphrey Carpenter, to ask:

Should we not wonder at the fact that a mind of such brilliance and imagination should be happy to be contained in the petty routine of academic and domestic life; that a man whose soul longed for the sound of waves breaking against the Cornish coast should be content to talk to old ladies in the lounge of a middle-class watering-place; that a poet in whom joy leapt up at the sight and smell of logs crackling in the grate of a country inn should be willing to sit in front of his own hearth warmed by an electric fire with simulated glowing coal?[2]

Yet it is precisely because Tolkien was a visionary that he was content to lead a life that to some, like poet W. H. Auden, appeared so appallingly staid. For Tolkien, Numenor was as real as, if not more real than, Oxford town. Although he himself may have disguised and felt ambivalent about that, psychologically Middle Earth existed as a literal place that he journeyed to. Whenever Tolkien found an unresolved mystery in the etymology of his Elvish languages or the history of the various races that populated his mythos, he would state, "I must find out" the answer, as would any intrepid empiricist seeking objective data in this world.

What is certain is that Tolkien's quest, often couched in the language of his discipline of philology, was to retrace the route of the development of modern consciousness back to that primal mind, "alive with mythological beings," which he termed Faery. Given the obviously visionary component of Tolkien's work, it is odd that more attention hasn't been given to this aspect of its nature.

Part of the problem may be Tolkien's presentation itself—he was not a man inclined toward the language and concepts of psychology, which he no doubt found superficial and "modern," and therefore degenerate. Consciousness, in the way it is being discussed here, was not a concept Tolkien would have been inclined to embrace, yet we can see a remarkable correspondence between Lewis-Williams's intensified trajectory and Tolkien's own descriptions of inner journeying, especially in his last creative work, "Smith of Wootton Major." In this deceptively simple tale, Tolkien left a veiled autobiographical account that might as well be, in the words of Tolkien scholar Paul Kocher, of "any practitioner of the

White Art who travels far 'from Daybreak to Evening' and in his old age comes home, tired, to hand his passport on to his successors."[3]

Considering that the old master laid aside work on his treasured *Silmarillion* to compose this guide to the realm of Faery, it is worthy of far closer attention than it is usually given.

Fortunately, along with the tale itself, Tolkien left an unpublished essay to accompany it—one very revealing of his intimate experience of the visionary realms his work records. In it, he attempts to describe the subjective experience of Faery.

> Faery represents at its weakest a breaking out (at least in mind) from the iron ring of the familiar—a constant awareness of the world beyond these rings. More strongly it represents love: a love and respect for all things, "inanimate" and "animate," and an unpossessive love of them as "other." This "love" will produce both *ruth* and *delight*. Things seen in its light will be respected, and they will also appear delightful, beautiful, wonderful, even glorious. Faery might be said to represent Imagination (without definition because taking in all the definitions of this word): esthetic, exploratory and receptive; and artistic; inventive, dynamic, (sub)creative. This compound—of awareness of a limitless world outside our domestic parish; a love (in ruth and admiration) for the things in it; and the desire for wonder, marvels, both perceived and conceived—this "Faery" is as necessary for the health and complete functioning of the Human as is sunlight for physical life.[4]

As Tolkien scholar Verlyn Flieger comments, "No great leap of imagination is needed in order to see that Tolkien was speaking from experience and that Faery was as necessary for his own spiritual health and complete functioning as sunlight for his physical life."[5]

In "Smith of Wootton Major," it emerges that Tolkien was deeply concerned with the issue of intensified consciousness. Indeed, he was struggling to define its workings, especially the experience of time alteration: "Entry into the 'geographical' bounds of Faery also involves entry into Faery Time. How does a mortal 'enter' the geographical realm of Faery? Evidently not in dream or illusion . . ."[6] Clearly, Tolkien is groping toward a model of consciousness, unaware that while existing as a geographical locale in the heart of the forest, Faery also can be interpreted by some as a function hardwired into the brain.*

Indeed, intensified consciousness appears to be the missing key to Tolkien's long-standing struggle to reconcile human and Faery time.

> There must be some way or ways of access from and to Faery . . . but it is also necessary that Faery and the world [of Men], though in contact, should occupy a different time and space, or occupy them in different modes. Thus, though it appears that Smith can enter Faery more or less at will, it is evident that it is a land or, world of unknown limits, containing seas and mountains; also it is plain that even during a brief visit (such as one on an evening walk) he can spend a great deal longer in Faery than his absence counts in the World; on his long journeys an absence from home of, say, a week

---

*"Trip reports" of Tolkien's contemporaries on the vast alterations in time and space lived within the orbit of extreme opium and cannabis intoxication, while not in tune with Tolkien's thinking, remind us that altered states of consciousness were as great an interest to his age as our own. Opium eater Thomas De Quincy reported visionary excursions in which he seemed to have lived a hundred years in a night. Lord Dunsany described such a fantastical, perilous hashish journey that it bears quoting at some length: "It takes one literally out of oneself. It is like wings. You swoop over distant countries and into other worlds. . . . I have seen incredible things in fearful worlds. As it is your imagination that takes you there, so it is only by your imagination that you can get back. Once out in the aether I met a battered, prowling spirit, that had belonged to a man whom drugs had killed a hundred years ago; and he led me to regions that I had never imagined; and we parted in anger beyond the Pleiades, and I could not imagine my way back. And I met a huge grey shape that was the Spirit of some great people, perhaps of a whole star, and I besought It to show me my way home. It pointed, and, speaking quite softly, asked me if I discerned a certain tiny light, and I saw a far star faintly, and then It said to me, "That is the Solar System," and strode tremendously on. Somehow I imagined my way back, and only just in time, for my body was already stiffening in a chair in my room; at last I could move one arm, and reached a bell, and at last a man appeared, and they got a doctor; and *he* said it was hashish poisoning, but it would have been all right if I hadn't met that battered, prowling spirit" (Dunsany, "The Hashish Man," 121–22).

is sufficient for exploration and experiences in Faery equivalent to months or even years.[7]

That Tolkien chose to mark the entrance to that enchanted forest of the tale with "a stone with a worn and faded carving of three trees and the inscription, *Welcō to þe Wode*"[8] is no accident. The Middle English *wode,* denoting both "wood" and "madness," as in the *wodewoses,* or wildmen of the medieval imagination, clearly points to something outside the realm of ordinary human experience.

"My symbol is not the underground," the usual entrance to the fairy world, Tolkien explains, "but the Forest: the regions still immune from human activities, not yet dominated by them. If Faery Time is at points contiguous with ours, the contiguity will occur in related points in space. . . . At certain points at or just within the Forest borders a human person may come across these contiguous points and there enter F. time and space—if fitted to do so."[9]

Given Tolkien's earlier evocations of the nonhuman sentience residing in the heart of forests (Tom Bombadil, the realm of Lothlórien), including those entirely vegetal (Old Man Willow, the ents and huorns of Fangorn), we may take the liberty of beginning to fill in the gap left in Tolkien's fecund mythopoeic imagination by that abstract phrase "points contiguous with ours" with Schultes's "resident plant divinity."

While Tolkien might be surprised to find his fantasy works compared with the enthnography of Amazonian Indians drinking psychoactive brews, his depictions of Aragorn's doctoring skills in the bush are distinctly shamanic and use a resident plant divinity for healing purposes. After Frodo is stabbed by the Morgul-blade on Weathertop, Aragorn sat with the weapon and "sang over it a slow song in a strange tongue. Then setting it aside, he turned to Frodo and in a soft tone spoke words the others could not catch. From the pouch at his belt he drew out the long leaves of a plant." This plant, *athelas,* he explains, "is a healing plant that the Men of the West brought to Middle Earth." He throws the leaves into boiling water, and the hobbits find "the fragrance of the steam refreshing, and those that were unhurt felt their minds calmed and cleared. . . .

Frodo felt the pain and also the sense of frozen cold lessen in his side."[10] The divine provenance of *athelas,* which responds especially to the hands of a rightful king, is made clearer when Aragorn performs a type of soul retrieval on Faramir, who has been gravely sickened by the Black Breath of the Nazgul. "Taking two leaves, he laid them on his hands and breathed on them,* and then he crushed them, and straightaway a living freshness filled the room, as if the air itself awoke and tingled, sparkling with joy."[11] The divine realm within the plant manifests, "like a memory of dewy mornings of unshadowed sun in some land of which the fair world in spring is itself but a fleeting memory."[12] Faramir awakens, summoned, and speaking softly, says, "My lord, you called me. I come. What does the king command?"[13]

To each his own with such medicine. In Aragorn's treatment of Lady Éowyn, who is not of Numenorian blood, she awakens not to breezes wafting from Valinor, the Undying Lands, but instead to a wind bearing the pure elements of Middle Earth: a "keen wind blew through the window, and it bore no scent, but was an air wholly fresh and clean and young, as if it had not before been breathed by any living thing and came new-made from snowy mountains high beneath a dome of stars, or from shores of silver far away washed by seas of foam."[14] Merry awakens, fittingly, to "the scent of orchards, and of heather in the sunshine full of bees"![15]

Aragorn's style of doctoring is in keeping with anthropologist Reichel-Dolmatoff's description of shamanic consciousness as the locale where fairy and human time meet. This "power of penetration" is

> the capacity to enter a trance and to undertake the magical flight that permits the payé to leave the biosphere and penetrate to another existential plane. A payé is at bottom a specialist in developing this rupture of levels in a spatial, ecstatic sense as well as in the sense of passing from one conceptual unit of time to another: ecstasy is

---

*Breath is used in shamanic practices to activate and direct the powers of the plant, as well as to imbue the medicine with the shaman's particular virtue. See the example of Casimero Mamallactas's breathing of the jaguar spirit into a patient as described later in this chapter.

equivalent to death and is, therefore, a process of acceleration of time.[16]

"Smith of Wootton Major" may, therefore, be justifiably read as it was intended: as a guide to those wishing to explore the realm of Faery.

The tale is set in motion by a traveler between realms, the Master Cook of a medieval town who, much like Bilbo, suddenly declares he is in need of a holiday and sets forth. Upon returning some months later, he has changed from a serious to a lighthearted man, and brings a quiet, but quick-witted, young apprentice back with him. He also bears a mysterious thing—a small silver star, a fay-star, for it turns out the adventurous Cook has been sojourning in Faery.

After a short time, the Cook departs, this time on a permanent holiday, leaving his apprentice Alf to eventually step into his role. The fay-star ends up being baked into a cake with a quaint little figure of a fairy queen on top, a cake that is traditionally offered to the select good children of the village at a feast held only once a generation. There, a boy named Smithson unknowingly ingests the fay star.

The entheogenic properties of the star take a while to manifest, but when they do, all the hallmarks of the gift of shamanic song and *seeing* are there. It comes at dawn months after the feast, on the boy's tenth birthday, when he hears the voice of wild nature, "the dawn-song of the birds beginning, growing as it came toward him, until it rushed over him, filling all the land around the house, and passed on like a wave of music into the West."[17]

Upon encountering, as if for the first time, nature's great song, the boy hears himself say, "It reminds me of Faery, but in Faery the people sing too." At that moment, just as may occur in the receiving of an icaro or other sacred song, "he began to sing, high and clear, in strange words that he seemed to know by heart." The star falls from his mouth into his hand, glistening and quivering. It begins to rise as if to fly away, but the boy intuitively claps his hand to his forehead, where the star remains for many years.

Smithson becomes Smith, in time, taking up his father's trade, and learns to sing the otherworldly virtue of the star he bears in his body, much like an Amazonian shaman will icarar the mariri of the plants into manifestation in the world. "His voice, which had begun to grow beautiful as soon as the star came to him, became ever more beautiful as he grew up. People liked to hear him speak, even if it was no more than a 'good morning.'" As well, his workmanship as a smith excelled, and along with kitchen tools, horseshoes, and pothooks, he made things for sheer delight: "he could work iron into wonderful forms that looked as light and delicate as a spray of leaves and blossom, but kept the strength of iron, or seemed even stronger." Of course, "he sang when he was making things of this sort; and when Smith began to sing those nearby stopped their own work and came to the smithy to listen."

The star has also given him the power to journey into the land of Faery, where we can see illustrated the work of harnessing the visionary capacity of the human mind.

Tolkien describes how, upon first entering Faery, Smith's "briefer visits he spent looking only at one tree or one flower" as he sought to bring into focus the new landscape. Smith also, as is often reported upon entering stage three of the intensified trajectory, experiences the sheer speed and wealth of the visionary landscape as bewildering, yet deeply transformative: "On longer journeys he had seen things of both beauty and terror that he could not clearly remember nor report to his friends, though he knew that they dwelt deep in his heart."

Eventually, Smith, as do all navigators into the primal mind, begins to take hold of the intensified trajectory, to master the art of transcosmological travel and preternatural sight. He perceives "things he did not forget, and they remained in his mind as wonders and mysteries that he often recalled." As well, he begins applying his otherworldly knowledge to this realm: "in time he could have forged weapons that in his own world would have had power enough to become the matter of great tales and be worth a king's ransom," but Smith does not fall into the trap of seeking power to dominate others. Instead, "it is not remembered that he ever forged a sword or a spear or an arrowhead."

Smith begins to go native. He is called Starbrow by the inhabitants of

Faery, and, as his explorations deepen, he becomes more intimate with the realm. Starbrow sees the elven mariners, "tall and terrible" with a "piercing light in their eyes," returning from battle in the realm of Unlight and falls on his face in fear as they march past him. He is rescued by a "blessed birch" tree, which sacrifices itself and weeps from all its shorn branches, to protect him from the Wind that is hunting the trespassing Starbrow. He beholds the King's Tree, the axis mundi, "springing up, tower upon tower, into the sky, and its light was like the sun at noon." Yet these visions come as gifts, not as a right, for, search as he will, he never encounters the King's Tree again.

Eventually, Starbrow penetrates to the heart of the realm, Evermorn, "where the green surpasses the green of the meads of Outer Faery as they surpass ours in the springtime," and brings a gift back to the human world. In this place, where wild nature is at its most concentrated and radiant, he dances with an elf maiden who puts a flower in his hair, a flower that never withers in our world and is treasured as an heirloom within Smith's family for many generations. Starbrow has begun to serve as a bridge.

So it is that Smith goes from passively experiencing marvelous visions to discovering his innate capacities in both worlds.

Starbrow finally *sees* the great pattern within which his life is woven, when he is summoned on a long journey to the Queen of Faery, who is a vision of nearly unbearable majesty. That is, until Starbrow recognizes her as the elf maiden he had danced with. "She smiled, seeing his memory, and drew toward him; and they spoke long together, for the most part without words, and he learned many things in her thought, some of which gave him joy, and others filled him with grief."

As often happens at the conclusion of a powerful visionary experience, Starbrow undergoes life review in light of the new knowledge he has received, and he recognizes the Queen's image in the little dancing figure on the cake that had contained the fay-star.

Rather than reducing the Queen's vast cosmic purport to a material cause, Smith recognizes the terrible folly of such reductionistic anthropomorphism, which distorts the great powers of the cosmos to the size of human miniatures, intellectual concepts, or hallucinations. Smith lowers his eyes in shame. Laughing, the Queen says, "Do not be grieved for me, Starbrow, nor too much ashamed of your own folk. Better a little doll, maybe, than no memory of Faery at all."

The Queen then gives Starbrow a message to deliver to the King, whose locale is unknown, and then strips away the last foreignness from his sight, giving him a native view: laying "her hand upon his head, a great stillness came upon him; and he seemed to be both in the World and in Faery, and also outside them and surveying them, so that he was at once in bereavement, and in ownership, and in peace." When Starbrow finally comes to, the field is empty, the Queen is gone, and he hears a distant echo of a trumpet in the mountains.

Bereaved, Starbrow finds his way back to the outskirts of Faery, where he encounters a hooded figure to whom he is inspired to entrust his message to the King. It is Alf the apprentice, the King in disguise. The King receives the fay-star back from Starbrow, who literally removes it from his forehead to pass on to the next generation, and Starbrow, now Smith, is given the option to serve as a bridge between the worlds one final time and choose his successor. By story's end, as a child of the next generation is illuminated by the fay-star, the cycle of interaction between Faery and the human world fully emerges, illustrating the vital, fertilizing, and hidden role of spiritual activity in the staid, and entropic, realm of human affairs.

As we can see, for Tolkien, ordinary consciousness is illuminated by the larger meanings bestowed on it by a divinely infused, sentient cosmos as experienced in the intensified trajectory, rather than reducible to hallucinatory epiphenomena of mere neurological activity. We are justified, therefore, in reading his final story as Tolkien's own passing on of the fay-star: as a guide to the realm of Faery.

The *Odyssey* is replete with characters who, like Starbrow, use "the possibilities of the intensified trajectory." In fact, in the *Odyssey* it may involve a pitched battle to extract information necessary for survival.

Marooned and starving on a small island off the Egyptian coast during his return home from Troy, Menelaus and his men must ambush and interrogate another master of animals figure, in this case a god named Proteus, in order to uncover the reasons for their misfortune. This "Old Man of the Sea" enjoys bedding down in deep hollow caves among his droves of seals, "like a shepherd with his flock" (*Odyssey* 4.464). Much as we have seen among the Greenland Eskimos, for whom when a tribe is unable to find enough seals and is threatened with famine a shaman will step in to violently negotiate with the mistress of animals, Menalaus and his men set their own ambush, disguised like Eskimo hunters in freshly stripped seal-skins. Proteus, eventually emerging from the sea makes his rounds, counts off his fat-fed seals, and then beds down to sleep. Menelaus and his men then spring their trap, and having pinioned him, must deal with the god's rapid-fire counterattack before the truth can be wrenched out of him: "First he shifted into a great bearded lion, and then a serpent—a panther—a ramping wild boar—a torrent of water—a tree with soaring branchtops—but we held on for dear life, braving it out" (*Odyssey* 4.512–15).

Finally, having navigated through the dancing layers of the entoptic and construal stages of the intensified trajectory, the god comes into focus and "burst[s] out into rapid-fire questions: 'Which god, Menelaus, conspired with you to trap me in an ambush? Seize me against my will? What on earth do you want?'" (*Odyssey* 4.519–21). Menelaus reveals his bad luck, and Proteus reveals, in turn, the etiology of Menelaus's dilemma, as well as the ritual that will allow him to sail home.

Menelaus's ordeal has much in common with the Native American vision quest, where, in the intensified trajectory, "the dreams in which spirits appear are more vivid than other dreams; the Shoshoni say that they hold your attention and you cannot awake until they are over." Proteus's rapid-fire transformations resemble aspects of shamanic visionary experiences: "Visions may be mercurial: for instance, a 'lightening spirit' may appear as a body of water, then like a human being, then like an animal." In addition, "Often frightening animals threaten suppliants, and they must brave them if their power-giving spirit animal is to appear." As Proteus becomes for Menelaus and his men, the spirit animal that finally reveals itself "will become the quester's animal-helper and source of his power."[18]

Such *seeing*, which is recognized among many native tribes, is achieved in a state the Shoshoni call *navushieip,* which denotes "both dreaming and waking . . . their divisions of the spectrum of consciousness thus accord dreaming the same status as waking for the reception of information."[19]

THE HEALING POWER OF ANIMAL TRANSFORMATION

Given the immense time depth and wide distribution of the practice of animal *becoming,* of what importance is such vestigial, indigenous experience for modern Westerners? Why should it be of any interest outside the arcane investigations of cognitive archaeologists, anthropologists, and depth psychologists?

Certainly, the capacity for animal transformation remains hardwired in the modern brain. American psychologist William James recorded this quaint account from a friend who had ingested a massive quantity of hashish.

> Directly I lay down upon a sofa there appeared before my eyes several rows of human hands, which oscillated for a moment, revolved and then changed into spoons. The motions were repeated, the objects changing to wheels, tin soldiers, lamp-posts, brooms, and countless other absurdities . . . there were moments of apparent lucidity, when it seems as if I could see within myself, and watch the pumping of my heart. A strange fear came over me, a certainty that I should never recover from the effects. . . . Suddenly there was a roar and a blast of sound . . . and I thought of a fox, and instantly I was transformed into that animal. I could distinctly feel myself a fox, could see my long ears and bushy tail, and by a sort of introversion felt that my complete anatomy was that of a fox.[20]

The stage of entoptic forms in the whirling wheels, tin soldiers, and brooms, the stage of construal in moments of lucidity and inner sight, and then the dramatic roar and blast that heralds the arrival of the animal ally, all fit admirably into Lewis-Williams's three-stage model.

Yet the impression left by this early account of animal *becoming* in the annals of Western psychology is that the informant has no preparation or cultural context by which to evaluate and integrate the experience. Rather like Professor Oesterreich with his meal of laurel leaves, it appears that James's informant was unable to derive much value from his experience. Without prayerful intention and a healthy veneration for the resident divinity of the plant being taken as sacrament, a psychedelic Mr. Toad's Wild Ride may be the result of such experimentation.

The possibility of harnessing the visionary state for profound healing purposes is suggested by Richard Grossinger in his discussion of the career of a Western shaman, a woman who was "viciously raped and then discarded for dead in a garbage can by her attacker." Devoting herself to "becoming a warrior and a healer, not out of rage or self-protection but as the only way to healing herself," this woman restored herself through her capacity to "mutate what had been done to her" through shamanic practices.[21]

As Grossinger insightfully comments:

> The patient of a shaman no doubt also has an "inner child," but that child is experienced as a raven or a wild bear and thus liberated to transmute, finally, into something larger than the neurosis. The so-called neurosis may have been no more than the unborn "shaman" within, careening toward its voice. No real growth can happen as long as the victim state requires either comforting or revenge. In fact the more deeply wounded the victim, the more powerful must be his or her potentiation in order to overcome the wound.[22]

The most intriguing, and harrowing, example of the therapeutic power of animal *becoming* I have ever encountered is Jaguar's.

I first met Jaguar at an NAC meeting. A tall, stocky man covered with tattoos in indigenous patterns and wearing rings in his ears, he was, and remains, reminiscent to me of Herman Melville's cannibal harpooner Queequeg, whose savage appearance belies his noble heart, and who makes a present of a shrunken head to Ishmael.

Jaguar had been among various indigenous tribes in the Amazon. As I came to know him better, I learned that in working with plant medicine traditions in the South and North, he had achieved such a remarkable degree of symbiosis with feline consciousness that he had, in negotiating with a deadly brain tumor, fundamentally changed his center of being from human to feline.

"My first vividly clear memory," he told me, "was at age three. I was sitting on my back porch watching my black cat fighting a dog through the fence. Walking down, I picked her up. Still in a fighting frenzy, she clawed me dozens of times. I could feel her pads bouncing off my face as my eyes filled with blood. One strike was dangerously close to my right eye, the only one that left a scar still easily visible today. To me, this scar symbolizes the moment my eyes opened and, like a newborn cub, I saw the world around me for the first time. She became my mother when she opened my face. At that point, my spirit could come into my body—but there was another spirit in there when I arrived."

As Jaguar describes it, that feline spirit indwelt in his human psyche, watching, as cats do, the events unfolding in Jaguar's young life. He often dreamt of jaguars and tigers, and thought Dr. Doolittle a most excellent character—and knew that he should learn how to talk to the animals, too. He also came to know that somewhere down the road he would have to make a choice to either be human or cat. "Your name is Jaguar," he was told. Yet he carried on his human life, not knowing what to do with that knowledge.

The turning point for Jaguar came when he was living in Australia in his early thirties, running the first body-piercing and tattoo shop entirely devoted to indigenous adornment, a time spent learning from the aboriginal elders and the Maori in Aeoteoroa, as well as absorbing all the information he could get on the Dayaks of Borneo, the shamans of Mentawai, and the Juaroni of Ecuador.

Jaguar dreamt that he had a brain tumor, awakening with painful headaches that lasted for a few weeks afterward. Eventually, he began to suffer infrequent blackouts. When his tumor was finally diagnosed, a brain surgeon informed him that he had only three months to a year to live without brain surgery.

But Jaguar stalled when he began to have nightmares and visions of dying on the operating table. Early in his martial arts training, he had learned that it was the strength of one's mind, not one's body, that made one a warrior. In the spirit of the words once inscribed on Viking swords, "Trust not in me if your own heart fails you," Jaguar knew he had to find another way to heal himself than solely through surgical intervention. "All you need to be is Jaguar," he kept hearing.

Jaguar was able to travel to Ecuador, where he participated in aya-huasca ceremonics with Casimero Mamallactas, an old Juaroni and Napo Runa* healer who delighted in his visitor's feline character. Casimero's grandfather—a jaguar, not a human—came in a vision and instructed Casimero to give Jaguar more medicine. Throughout the evening, the wry old man kept calling Jaguar up to drink, laughing that, "We'll breathe more jaguar spirit into him!"†

Jaguar started to connect with the "original spirit," the human self, through his feline self. The human self, he understood, had been through a lot of suffering: "One of the things I got from entering into conversation with that spirit was it felt like it had been stillborn, born dead. Metaphorically, it was like walking into your house and there's somebody on the floor in a heap. You have a sense they're all right, they're not in any physical danger, but you don't know what to do, because they're not responding." It became clear around the time of his diagnosis with the tumor that the human had been through a lot of suffering and was ready to return to where he had come from.

Not much later, upon completing his training as a Bikram yoga teacher, Jaguar started to black out and experience spasms, as if his brain were clenching. After he had been teaching for about four months, an MRI

---

*The Juaroni tribe are those mentioned above, who believe themselves to be reborn as jaguars, and so withdraw into the forest to undergo their transformation when death approaches.

†Casimero's breathing of jaguar spirit into Jaguar concretely enacts the most archaic meaning of the Greek term *psyche,* originally derived from the verb *psychein,* "to breathe" or "to blow." In the Amazon, this practice of breathing spirit or soul into another is still practiced among the traditional cultures.

image revealed that the tumor had tripled in size. Jaguar became aware that he was beginning to cross a kind of event horizon. He determined to face his death, if it was the will of the Creator, open-eyed and without shrinking.

Jaguar began to understand his brain tumor in a traditional Amazonian way—part of the reason the brain tumor had come was become he wasn't embracing who he was. "The last thing you want to be is a shaman," Jaguar said. "You run from it. And, of course, it usually comes down to a life-or-death situation before you make the choice."

"A shaman never comes into his medicine alive," he had been told in Peru. Jaguar, now in the midst of the crisis, intuited that he had to choose to assume his full identity, as he had been told in a spirit vision years before: "Your name is Jaguar—this is all you need in the world."

When Jaguar had reached the juncture where he could look down and see one foot in the other world and one foot in the physical world, he found the NAC. He was put in touch with the roadman John Nighthorse Tyler, son of Henry Tyler, who invited him to a peyote ceremony on Easter weekend where he also gave him a few Arapaho doctoring sessions.

"In one night, in that ceremony, I went through twenty years of mental/emotional work. I got well like fifteen or twenty times that night—I was constantly throwing up. A subsequent MRI, from about four months afterward, revealed the tumor reverse-tripled—it shrank to its original size in one night."

Deeply impressed and grateful, Jaguar sponsored three NAC prayer meetings over the next four years. Although the medical doctors had told him that he could continue to have symptoms, such as migraines, blackouts, and seizures, he displayed none of those after that Easter meeting with his adopted uncle, John Nighthorse Tyler.

As Jaguar continued working with the medicine, his encounters with cats deepened. In one tipi, he saw spirit cats who would enter two by two and sit in front of him. Jaguar would ask, "What are you guys doing here?" They would simply answer, "We came to see you, to sit with you." When the mountain lion spirits came, they said, "We saw you when you were a child." Jaguar had the ancient image of the baby put in the basket and set adrift in the river, unaware of the world around, or even that it was afloat. "They communicated to me that they had seen me alone in the world, unaware of the potential monsters around me."

"We had our eyes on you," the mountain lions told him, "and when the moment came, when we could, we touched you with intelligence and intention. We touched your body and marked you as ours. You belong to us." Other times, mountain lions would literally creep up and sit next to other ceremonial sites, sometimes startling participants by peering in.

Nonetheless, he could still feel a little physical tension, like the proverbial pea under the mattress, remaining at the base of his brain. Bob Boyll, Jaguar's adopted uncle who had also been working with him for some years, told him cancer is a spirit and it is possible to communicate and negotiate with it, just like any other spirit. In his third meeting, Jaguar succeeded. After several attempts at communication, the tumor told him, "I heard you. I'm leaving."

There were nine roadpeople and thirteen indigenous nations represented at that meeting. That ceremony was especially memorable, however, for the permeability of consciousness, the sheer joyful interplay among the elements and many beings that took place there. The animal nations, for example, were strongly present. Jaguar relates, "We were building a sweat lodge in the rain and the backyard bordered on a pasture. At a certain point, I felt something and turned to look. Every single cow in that pasture was right there, next to us, against the fence, pushing their faces against the wire, trying to check out what we were doing with the sweat lodge. I reached out to pet one of the cow's noses and it licked my hand."

In the morning after the ceremony, a red-tailed hawk flew in from the east, circled clockwise around the tipi and then flew back to the east again. An osprey sat in the tree right by the tipi. "My auntie," Jaguar said, "when she was bringing in the morning water, right before she stepped through the door into the tipi looked into the sky. A 'V' of geese was directly above, so as she entered the tipi they were flying the same path above her."

As Jaguar explains it, the old ways down South have it that the morning after a ceremony we can read the metaphors present in nature to interpret the outcome of the ceremony. If it's a dark, rainy day it probably didn't go so well. "It had been raining like crazy, for days before and right up to the start of the ceremony. Torrential, steel-gray clouds dominated the sky." In the morning portion of the ceremony, he looked up through the hole in the tipi and saw vivid blue sky. "I said, 'Okay, Creator, I need to know that you're with me in this prayer in a real way. I need to see that. I need a sign.'" Feeling a rainbow happening outside, he said, "I need to see a rainbow, Creator, so I know that it's going to work out for me, that I'm not going to die." His partner at the time, who had passed the night outside the tipi, came in soon after, and, approaching Jaguar, grabbed him and said, "There's a rainbow outside the tipi! First, it was covering the whole tipi, then it was on the left side, and then someone got a photo of the tipi, with the rainbow coming off the right side!"

With such a confabulation of elements and beings of the sentient cosmos at the site of Jaguar's healing, it's no surprise he's in excellent health these days. Reflecting on his healing process and the role symbiosis with feline consciousness had to play in it, he says, "What saved my life was the medicine, for sure. The plant intelligence saved my physical, mental, and emotional bodies. But it's my lifelong connection with the cats that made that healing possible. They've been protecting this body and mind, this intelligence, all the way from day one so I could get that healing.

"The big question for me is," Jaguar concluded, "in the face of the wild cats' shrinking habitats and dwindling populations, how can I use this cat medicine for their benefit?

There are mysterious forces afoot in Jaguar's healing, the same ones we see constellated in the prophetic vision of Black Elk (1863–1950), the Oglala Sioux shaman whose remarkable life story was set down by the poet John Neihardt in the 1930s. His account reminds us of how deeply woven together the themes of animal *becoming,* the gifts of plants, and human survival in clans run in indigenous prophecy. For Black Elk, to be animal is to be attuned to one's clan, to follow the path of the one-hearted.

Black Elk's initiatory vision, coming at the tender age of nine when white civilization was overspilling its boundaries and posing a grave threat to his people, is Dantean in scale and remarkably mature in theme.

Rooted in Lakota traditional beliefs, it is clearly another spring feeding the greater stream of indigenous prophetic voices that reckon with the emerging, and far deeper, threat to human culture on Earth.

In Black Elk's vision, he and his people must make a series of four ascents through mountainous terrain. In the first he sees a blessed continuance of his clan, of the "generations I should know . . . as the long line climbed, all the old men and women raised their hands, palms forward, to the far sky yonder and began to croon a song together, and the sky ahead was filled with clouds of baby faces."[23]

That night, they camp in a sacred circle. In the center stands the holy tree, and the land surrounding them is green.

In the next morning's ascent, he sees before him "the people changed into elks and bison and all four-footed beings and even into fowls, all walking in a sacred manner on the good red road together. And I myself was a spotted eagle soaring over them." The exuberance of this vision of animal *becoming*, reflecting the deep-seated well-being and happiness of his people, gives way when "the marching animals grew restless and afraid that they were not what they had been, and began sending forth voices of trouble."

Looking down, Black Elk sees that "leaves were falling from the holy tree." A voice reminds him to remember his spiritual gifts, "for thenceforth your people walk in difficulties."[24]

The following morning, much as in the Hopi prophecy of the road of the two-hearted, the people become disheartened and purposeless, not wanting to continue on but unable to stay. "All the animals and fowls that were the people ran here and there, for each one seemed to have his own little vision that he followed and his own rules; and all over the universe I could hear the winds at war like wild beasts fighting."[25]

Arriving at the next summit, Black Elk finds that the sacred circle is broken, "like a ring of smoke that spreads and scatters." The holy tree seems to be dying, and the birds have all fallen silent.

Upon the fourth morning, the Voice speaks like one weeping, "Look there upon your nation."

Black Elk sees they are "all changed back to human, and they were thin, their faces sharp, for they were starving. Their ponies were only hide and bones, and the holy tree was gone." Bereft of their spiritual gifts, their immersion in a vital, living cosmology, Black Elk's people are reduced to the merely human, to physical and spiritual starvation.[26]

Then comes a sacred man carrying a spear, painted red all over his body, who walks into the center of the people and rolls on the ground. When he stands, he has metamorphosed into a fat bison, and where the animal stood, a sacred herb springs up, "right where the tree had been in the center of the nation's hoop."

Much as peyote came to help reinvigorate and unify the dislocated and imperiled cultures of the Plains Indians, as Black Elk watches, the herb grows, bearing "four blossoms on a single stem—a blue, a white, a scarlet, and a yellow—and the bright rays of these flashed to the heavens."

Black Elk understands. From the spirit that gave the gift of the bison, then being exterminated in the wild by the white invaders, comes a new gift, a plant that can give new strength. "For the people all seemed better, and the horses raised their tails and neighed and pranced around, and I could see a light breeze going from the north among the people like a ghost; and suddenly the flowering tree was there again at the center of the nation's hoop where the four-rayed herb had blossomed."[27]

The forces of history in Black Elk's time overpowered his sacred vision: "I did not know then how much was ended. . . . A people's dream died there. It was a beautiful dream. The nation's hoop is broken and scattered. There is no center any longer, and the sacred tree is dead."[28]

Yet Jaguar's healing, for this writer at least, demonstrates that the sacred tree continues to flourish. Indeed, David Monongue, in transmitting the butterfly kachina song to Boyll, explained that the butterfly's wings express the colors of the leaves of the Tree of Life, and the song is a prayer for the completion of the Great Purification and for the blooming of the tree again.

"The tree is now ailing and withered," he told Boyll, "but you may live to see the flowering. I know I won't, but I want you to have this to sing in anticipation of that day."

EIGHT

DESCENT to HADES

Traditional people, and I think the people of the Paleolithic had, very probably, two concepts that change our vision of the world: the concept of fluidity and the concept of permeability. Fluidity means the categories that we have, man, woman, horse, tree, etc., can shift. A tree may speak. A man can get transformed into an animal and the other way around, given certain circumstances. The concept of permeability is that there are no barriers, so to speak, between the world where we are and the world of spirits. A shaman, for example, can send his or her spirit to the world of the supernatural or can receive the visit of supernatural spirits. When you put those two concepts together, you realize how different life must have been for those people from the way we live now.

PREHISTORIAN JEAN CLOTTES

If the breadth and depth of the *Odyssey* make it akin to an archaeological site, richly strewn with the remains of prehistoric lore, the most vertiginous glimpse the poem gives into the time depths of the shamanic practices of Western Europe is Odysseus's journey into the realm of Hades.

Odysseus's summoning of the blind prophet Tiresias in the land of the dead has long been recognized as shamanic in character by Homeric scholars, yet none, to my knowledge, have sought to understand it more profoundly by considering how Odysseus's descent may be a reflection of ancestral, and contemporary, shamanic practices.

It is Circe who breaks the news to Odysseus that to complete his journey home to Ithaca, he must first go to Hades, where he must consult the sage Tiresias, who retains his oracular power even in the land of the dead.

Odysseus accomplishes this task by setting sail and surrendering his craft to the North Wind, which carries him beyond the reach of the sun to a place where the rivers of the underworld converge at a grove sacred to Persephone. There, Odysseus tells his men to await him and, entering the grove, digs a trench, over which he slits the throat of a black ram provided to him for that purpose by Circe and allows the trench to fill with blood.* He then sits and waits, sword in hand, to keep in order the coming of the spirits. The shades of the dead, drawn by the blood, which has the power to restore to them their faculties of speech and emotional intelligence (*phrenes* and *thymos*), gradually manifest and approach to drink.

First to come is Elpennor, a crew member who had fallen to his death the morning of their departure and was left unburied in the main hall of Circe's palace. Not having completed his transmigration, Elpennor still possesses the power of speech and recognition: he demands of Odysseus burial and proper funerary rites to fully enter the underworld, which Odysseus promises him. Elpennor is a grim reminder of the role predatory animism has in shamanic practices—as well as evidence of the great time depth of Homer's oral tradition.† The likely truth, smoothed over by Homer's polished narrative, is that Elpennor was sent to blaze the trail

---

*"That's because he didn't have ayahuasca!" laughed Flores, upon hearing this account.
†The Hades episode has a particular architecture that bards could adapt and improvise on, while leaving its deep structure intact. In such a way, much as a Celtic sacred well and Roman temple pillars could underlie the foundation of a medieval Christian church, the original elements of the Hades narrative are discernible within the structure of Homer's account.

Odysseus follows: he is the human sacrifice that opens the way into the Nightland.*

Elpennor is followed by Odysseus's mother, who, as the stunned and grief-stricken Odysseus holds her back from drinking the blood, crouches mute and blind beside the trench. Finally, the sage Tiresias appears, boisterously making his way through the flitting and scurrying shades. Telling Odysseus to lower his sword, the sage drinks the blood and, his voice awakened, booms out his prophecy. Afterward, he tells Odysseus that he can speak with any of the dead he wishes to—all he has to do is allow them to approach the blood and drink.

This starts the long, famous series of interviews conducted by Odysseus in the underworld, which begin with reunions at the site of the trench but rapidly lose a sense of physical locale to turn into transcorporal voyaging and pure *seeing,* as Odysseus beholds the great archetypal figures (much as the Tukano *see* the anaconda, the stick rattle of the Sun Father, the First Maloca, First Woman, First Dance, and other sacred figures,[1] of his own culture's cosmovision: Tantalus, Sisyphus, Heracles, and a long parade of august queens of earlier ages. Finally, reminding us that "liaising with the spirits is not without danger, for transference between worlds is itself full of risk and there is always a chance that the shaman may not be able to reenter his or her own cosmic space,"[2] Odysseus is seized by fear that Persephone will send up a Medusa head from the depths, turning his psyche to stone. Wrenching himself out of a trance, he hastens forth from the grove and orders his men to cast off and set sail for the kind sun and the land of the living.

While the instructions Odysseus receives from Tiresias are valuable, the reader intuits that it is more the "penetrative power" with which Odysseus faces the forces governing his fate that breaks Poseidon's watery grip on him. Like a planet reaching its farthest orbit from the sun, Odysseus reaches his aphelion in Hades. Although many long years of hardship still separate him from Ithaca, having made his descent, his trajectory is afterward set once more toward home.

---

*I wish to thank Dr. Daniel Melia of the UC-Berkeley Celtic Studies department for pointing out to me the possible origin of Elpennor's death in the practice of Neolithic human sacrifice.

One of the obstacles to correctly interpreting the shamanic nature of Odysseus's journey may have been Mircea Eliade's huge emphasis on *magic flight,* which classicist E. R. Dodds describes as "the liberation of the shaman's spirit, which leaves his body and sets off on a mantic journey."[3] Such an emphasis can be misleading, for the shamanic practices of the Amazon correspond far better with Homer's narrative than do the Siberian. As religious scholar and practicing vegetalista Steve Beyer points out, "There seem to be three modes of interaction with the spirits: the shaman can travel to where the spirits are—the classic soul flight; the shaman can summon the spirits to where the shaman is; or the spirits can enter and take possession of the shaman's body."[4] Whereas scholars have studied the first and last of these, few have focused on the predominant mode in the Amazon—summoning.

Just as Odysseus takes his seat before the trench to order the coming of the dead and conducts interviews to gather the information he requires, a vegetalista shaman, using icaros, will summon the spirits to work as protectors and doctors as he directs them. Among the titles given to such shamans is *banco;* that is, a "seat" or "bench."

For Juan Flores, a *banco muraya* is the master of the plants and animals on the land, and is accompanied by the *banco puma,* the spotted jaguar of the jungle.[5] As the honorific *banco* indicates, Flores establishes the seat around which the spirits will congregate, summoning first the spirits of the land, such as those of the medicinal trees and his ally animals; then of the water, such as those of the giant boa, sirenas, and the black jaguar; and finally of space, such as Jesus, Buddha, the Virgin Mary, the ancient Incans, and other doctor curanderos. Only then does he begin his healing work. Then as the insubstantial pageant fades at the ceremony's conclusion, Flores laughs and smokes mapachos, joking about the beauties and terrors traversed that evening.

Beyer notes as well that, like Flores, his teachers "do not explicitly go to the land of the spirits, nor do they interact with plant or animal spirits on their journeys, in order to heal their patients. To do that, they call the spirits to the place of the ceremony."[6]

Yet, just as Odysseus does when his business is completed with Tiresias and his deceased kin, traveling and *seeing* the mythic sights of Hades, vegetalista shamans may transcorporate after the ceremony's work is done. Then, "they journey to *see*—distant landscapes, far galaxies, vast hospitals, convocations of shamans. They do not travel on business."[7] And, as Odysseus or any good tourist does, they often will recount stories of their journeys afterward, as Flores did one night, describing the wonderful chacra, or subsistence garden, of the Chulla Chaqui he visited, and detailing its features to me.

Another important indigenous feature of the Hades episode is the overlapping or, rather, interpenetration of physical and spiritual topography. Odysseus must physically journey to where the spirits are, in a locale such as Persephone's grove, remote and terrible, half in this world and half out of it, yet, like the lunar surface, accessible to mortals.

This is solidly in the tradition of the vision quest, in which the applicant attempts to make his or her consciousness permeable to the spirit realm, especially by seeking out locales of special power to facilitate this opening.

As Flores related to us, "I like to find where the strongest spirits are so I can learn from them. Spirits like to live in the mountains and in the most silent places of the jungle. They don't like noise. So I would go to these places to learn from them and receive teaching, but the communication is by means of the plants, the diets—when one drinks ayahuasca, the spirits come to talk."[8]

One such locale that Flores visited, deep in the jungle three days' voyage by boat from the town of Santa Rosa de Masisea, was accessible only once a day when a canyon opened in the mountain to permit entrance to a hidden lagoon. There, drinking ayahuasca, he sat and waited along with the others in the party until the sound of a deep throbbing in the waters heralded the arrival of a great vessel,* a ship of iron, filled with specialists in medicine, emerging from the depths of the lake. Much as Odysseus seeks in his interview with Tiresias, Flores wished to "encounter

---

*See Pablo Amaringo's luminous depiction of this spirit boat, the *Aceropunta*, as Vision 20 of his *Ayahuasca Visions* (Luna and Amaringo, 86).

the ancient doctors and curanderos that exist on the other side as spirits in order to converse with them, to find out how they saw me as a curandero. I simply wanted to learn. If they had not accepted me, I wouldn't have returned to this life."[9]

In a similar progression to Odysseus's moving from interviewing the mortal deceased to a transcorporal *seeing* of the archetypal, mythic realm, Flores first encountered the great healers of the past from his tribe, the Ashaninca, and conversed with them. Then he saw the mythic sirenas, and, moving into pure *seeing,* beheld Manco Capac and Mama Ocllo, the first Incans to emerge from the depths of Lake Titicaca to bring the arts of civilization to humanity.

While the ethnographic parallels between ancient Greek and contemporary Amazonian shamanistic journeying are compelling, we must go a step further and ask: What was the nature of the archaic experience that is enshrined in Homer's poem, an experience so profound that it left such a deep mark on our collective memory?

A strong clue lies in the painted caves of prehistoric Europe, the oldest of which date from 32,000 BCE. From their ever-dark caverns come awesome visions of subterranean animal powers, the primordial stuff of myth that anthropologist Claude Lévi-Strauss called "a story about the time when humans and animals did not yet distinguish themselves from each other."[10]

There we find imagery that strongly suggests a similar interpenetration of spiritual and physical topography. In Paleolithic peoples' descents into the subterranean realms, it seems likely they encountered an "immanent" world of spirit, one "interdigitating with the material world, as well as separate from it,"[11] and that they attempted to make that world visible in the breathtaking art that adorns their caves. This visionary landscape of the spirit world was "given topographical materiality" in their physical passage into the depths of the caverns, as the flickering of their oil lamps illuminated the "embellishing images" that "blazed a path into the unknown."[12]

Embellishing images leading into darkness also characterizes the shades of the dead that Odysseus encounters in Hades. The Ancient

Greeks used the word *eidola,* "image," to describe the burned-out husks of once-living humans, ghosts akin to the image we behold in our household mirror—without inherent substance, yet real enough. Try to embrace them, as Odysseus does the eidola of his mother, and your arms will pass right through. Much as the visions recorded in the Paleolithic caves, these images dwelling in Hades, latent in the blind night, await restoration to life through the shaman's vital force, his capacity to *see.*

While the pioneering vision quests of the Paleolithic were most likely conducted in deep caves, over time, the walls became populated with iconography and subtly transformed into shrines. As the permeable consciousness of shamanic states became more ritualized and developed as a social function, Lewis-Williams theorizes that more and more truth value was given to visions received in the extremest depths. Such primacy of depth, and the celebration of ascetic hardiness on the part of the shaman/ priests to achieve it, suggests how the sanctified role of Tiresias, as the voice of oracular authority in the depths of Hades, could have evolved.

These subterranean cathedrals, then, in which early Europeans conducted their vision quests, not only served as a cultural product that made visible the Upper Paleolithic cosmos in art, but also as a physical enactment of the psychic passage through the stages of trance.

As described by Lewis-Williams, "the sensory deprivation afforded by the remote, silent and totally dark chambers, such as the Diverticule of the Felines in Lascaux and the Horse's Tail in Altamira, induces altered states of consciousness. In their various stages of altered states, questers sought, by sight and touch, in the folds and cracks of the rock face, visions of powerful animals. It is as if the rock were a living membrane between those who ventured in and one of the lowest levels of the tiered cosmos; behind the membrane lay a realm inhabited by spirit animals and spirits themselves, and the passages and chambers of the caves penetrated deep into that realm."[13]

Certainly, if one gazes into the paintings of the lions in Chauvet cave long enough, one realizes they are not, in fact, paintings. They are the lions themselves, or rather, the imprint of the animal spirit on human consciousness. With no separation between the artist and his subject, even gazing on

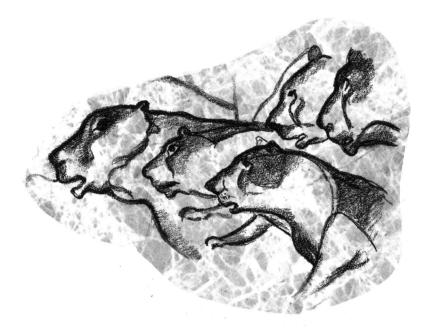

Fig. 8.1. The lions of Chauvet cave

the images through the medium of photographs provides a glimpse into the permeability of consciousness of the Paleolithic artist/shamans.

In fact, the living quality of the images, the sense of being surrounded by spirits, in much the same way as Odysseus encounters spirits in Hades, was reported by Werner Herzog, who recalls that during their hours of filming his documentary *Cave of Forgotten Dreams* inside Chauvet cave, "Sometimes we were overcome by a strange, irrational sensation, as if we were disturbing the Paleolithic people in their work. It felt like eyes upon us. This sensation occurred to some of the scientists and also the discoverers of the cave. It was a relief to surface again above ground."[14]

One scientist interviewed by Herzog said when he first entered Chauvet cave it was such a powerful experience that every night he dreamt of lions and passed each day in emotional shock. He finally chose not to return underground for a time in order to absorb what he had been experiencing. When asked if he dreamt of paintings of lions or real lions, he answered, "Both," and said he wasn't afraid. Rather, he had "a feeling of powerful things. Of deep things. A way to understand things that is not a direct way."[15]

Perhaps the most beautiful metaphoric expression of the Dreamtime quality of these caves, where the fiction of the separation of events in time melts away and simultaneity in spirit reveals itself, is to be encountered in the footprints of a wolf and a boy standing next to one another, found in the depths of Chauvet cave. The scientists who study the cave do not know if the wolf was walking with the boy, if the wolf was stalking the boy (or vice versa), or even if the footprints are from the same moment in time or separated by thousands of years. And yet, from a more indigenous perspective, like the cave paintings, the footprints themselves could be seen as direct imprints of the realm of spirit—a perfect symbol of human and animal walking together in the eternity of Dreamtime.

So, one can make a very strong argument that in these caves we can see traces of experience very similar to Odysseus's journey into Hades: shamanic journeying through a visionary landscape permeable to spirit, projected onto the psychic tableau of cavernous geological formations, dissolving into greater and greater depths as full immersion in stage three of the intensified trajectory is sought in the deepest chambers.

With the passing generations, the evidence strongly suggests that visionary journeys migrated from the Paleolithic caves to Neolithic burial chambers such as Newgrange, where, based on archaeological work on these prehistoric sites (and some vigorous historical reconstruction), we can now envision the more direct predecessors of Odysseus as

> an elite group of Neolithic religious functionaries, perhaps shamans accompanied by a chieftain or tribal elders, sitting with the ancestral bones within the passage grave, experiencing altered states of consciousness. Perhaps their aim would have been communing with the spirits of the dead through the medium of visual, aural, and other sensory hallucinations. Or, with their supernatural abilities activated in trance they could listen to the spirits and join with the ancestors in the Otherworld by temporarily leaving their physical bodies. . . . The bones, especially the skulls, might have provided the frameworks for the appearance of animated spectral forms; the walls of the chamber might have extended to mighty proportions while

flickering with kaleidoscopic energy patterns before opening up as portals into the fearsome underworld of the dead, or glorious heavenworlds. These may have been glimpsed first in the form of vistas; then the spirits of the ritual participants would have journeyed into those realms, perhaps guided by the ancestral spirits associated with the bones preserved in the chamber.[16]

Odysseus's account seems to combine both Paleolithic and Neolithic elements. As did Paleolithic people descending into the caves, he must travel to a sacred, wild, and remote locale where the human may interpenetrate with the spirit realm; as with Neolithic people, his visions are of a more settled, agricultural, and humanly populated realm.

Like the dying off of the herds of wild aurochs and wooly mammoths, prides of lions, and shambling, solitary cave bears, first from the land itself and then from ancestral memory, the master of animals and other Paleolithic divine figures also receded, gradually anthropomorphizing into urbane human forms—albeit some still with hooves and horns and animal metamorphoses—in which we now know them.

Except, that is, for the Wildman. Cyclopes continued to haunt the margins of the world.

NINE

BOUND TO THE MAST

Initiation
versus Addiction

Be not afeard. The isle is full of noises,
Sounds, and sweet airs, that give delight and hurt not.
Sometimes a thousand twangling instruments
Will hum about mine ears, and sometimes voices,
That, if I then had waked after long sleep,
Will make me sleep again; and then, dreaming,
The clouds methought would open and show riches
Ready to drop upon me, that when I waked
I cried to dream again.

CALIBAN IN WILLIAM SHAKESPEARE'S
THE TEMPEST

Some years ago, as part of our apprenticeship in the vegetalista tradition, Susana and I worked at Takiwasi, a center for the treatment of drug and alcohol addiction located in the high jungle plateau of the San Martín Province of Peru. Founded by the physicians Jacques Mabit and Rosa Giove, the center combines contemporary Western therapies with the indigenous healing practices of the Amazon rain forest—including rigorous ceremonies with the visionary plant ayahuasca. The center has an unusually high rate of complete recuperation among its clients.

Deeply engaged as we were in the addicts' struggles to unravel the fate that had consumed their lives, I occasionally stood in contemplation of a work of art hanging in the office of the director of the center. In the oil painting, a young Native American wearing head feathers stares, head lowered, at his extended, upturned arm. A rubber tube is tightly bound around his forearm, and in his hand is a syringe, hovering over a swollen vein. As he prepares to shoot up, he is unaware that a Buddhist deity, its face filled with compassion, is gazing down on him.

The juxtaposition of images—the indigenous warrior, the modern technology of addiction, the religious iconography—was disturbing. Was it honoring the path of addiction as spiritual? Was it offering hope in the bleakest, dark night of the soul? Or was it, enigmatically, doing both?

In this chapter I wish to offer some musings on initiation and its shadow, addiction, as those human experiences can be reckoned with as *reflected* within the mythic structures of the *Odyssey*. In treating certain features of the poem, such as the Sirens' song, as metaphoric for addiction, I am not attempting to reduce their otherworldly essence to a physiological/psychological condition. Quite the opposite. I am attempting to view the phenomenon of addiction from a larger framework of understanding, to offer a new approach to a dilemma that has proved largely intractable to rational ways of thinking.

Over half a century ago, the famous psychoanalyst C. G. Jung pointed out that the deeper craving of the addict's soul is not the substance itself, nor its effects: it is a profound "thirst for wholeness," the natural drive of the psyche to heal from an illusory separation from the web of life.

The very drive, in short, that underlies shamanic practices.

Filled as the *Odyssey* is with highly intoxicating, addictive, and benumbing substances, which sorely tempt Odysseus and his crew to abandon their homeward journey, it is worth considering the character traits that Odysseus shares with mature shamans—those who also display a capacity to enter into highly perilous regions of the psyche without being seduced and entrapped within them.

Unlike the addict, for whom the voyage into the soul becomes marooned in a substance, such as heroin or alcohol, and his life outside the drug's feigned experience of intimacy a hell of dwindling air and light, the mature shaman, having passed through the agonies of his initiation ordeals, enters into greater spaciousness and beauty.

The addicts undergoing treatment at Takiwasi had embarked on a shamanic path of self-healing. They had chosen (with whatever actual degree of understanding) to confront themselves in the profoundest way. Like Odysseus bearing the curse of Poseidon, they had chosen to journey into the soul's abyss in order to unravel the fate that held them captive.

In this, they shared something with the ancient Greeks, for whom a fundamental act of heroism (and diagnosis) in an otherwise kaleido-scopically shifting world of spirits and powers was to seize one's thread of fate. The actual spinning of one's destiny by the three Fates, or Moirae, is evocative of the twisting strands of proteins in DNA. As Clotho, the "Spinner," spun the thread of life, Lakhesis, the "Apportioner of Lots," measured it, assigning genetic dispositions. Finally, Atropos (who, we recall, was to bestow her name on the atropine alkaloids of the Solanaceae family), "She who cannot be turned," determined the moment of death by cutting the thread.

While the thread encoded the fundamental information of a person's incarnation, there was wiggle room. Choice in how to live out one's fate still remained open, and divinity could also intervene in an individual's fate, to some degree. In this way, freedom and fate inextricably inter-mingled. While the Moirae themselves appear as terrible, white-robed old women, stern and unmovable as Victorian spinster aunts, there are accounts of gods wheedling concessions out of them by getting them drunk![1]

What this reflects is that, for the Ancients, the nature of existence was, while interpretable, fundamentally unknowable at its source. In Germanic and Nordic warrior culture, a similar perspective led to a mar-velous heroic existentialism, yet we see the heroes and heroines of the

Odyssey adopting a more heuristic approach to the endless dimensions of existence. True, as with Chinese boxes, one could never arrive at a final box where an ultimate reality awaits discovery within, yet the answers for the present exigencies *did* lie within one of those layers of reality and could occasionally be uncovered with boldness and determined inquiry.

What the character of Odysseus and other figures in the literature of ancient Greek culture demonstrates is an adaptive stance toward divinity: not faith in God—they revered, but didn't trust, Zeus!—but faith in the fundamental *logos* of the universe.

Such a perspective on existence shares much with indigenous world-views. This sort of vertiginous openness to inquiry among Amazonian shamans was first revealed to us by Juan Flores in a conversation we had while preparing plant medicines we had just gathered in the jungle. Flores, seated on a tree stump with an ax resting on his knees, suddenly posed a question to us in classic Socratic fashion: "You both are very educated people. Tell me, is there something that God doesn't know?"

Coming from a vegetalista who incorporated many Catholic elements into his ceremonies, this was a disconcerting question. While we both cast about for possible answers, Juan pressed us further: "God is the creator of everything, right? So if he's the creator, shouldn't he know everything?"

As Susana explained how Vedanta philosophy would respond to such a question, I studied Flores's expression, trying to discover if he was laying some trap for us. But he looked genuinely interested in our responses. Finally, he asked us, "If we cannot know what lies outside of ourselves, how can God know what lies outside himself?" Juan then got up and walked away, leaving us to contemplate the Chinese box structure of the universe.

Considering that Flores saw ayahuasca as the university of the jungle, within which one could travel to distant times and study the art of, say, the ancient Egyptians, or could commune with ancient and powerful spirits—indeed, could be inhabited by them—or travel to other dimensions of space, it is probably no surprise that he, like the ancient Greeks, was willing to embrace a radically inquiring stance toward existence without denying the sacredness of the cosmos.

As has been recognized since most ancient times, "In poison there is psychic." A plant doctor transforms, or is transformed by, the poison* he takes into his body as medicine, but doesn't fall under its spell. Such power can be wielded for good or evil (thus the ambivalence expressed by the Romans over Odysseus's amoral cunning). Whatever the outcome, the shaman must drink the poison his fellow men rightly fear to imbibe, and the outcome is a character his fellow men are right to distrust—but are foolish to persecute.

In my time among practitioners of shamanic, indigenous medicine, I have come to observe three traits that characterize both Odysseus and those medicine women and men who live balanced, innovative lives into a highly functional old age: an adaptive, disciplined strength of mind; accompanied by an unquenchable thirst for knowledge; tempered by a profound attitude of veneration.

A fine illustration of this sort of strength of mind is shown in a little scene between the newly reunited Odysseus and his son Telemachus.

As they enter the darkened hall of the palace on Ithaca, Pallas Athena goes striding before them, lifting a golden lamp that casts a dazzling brilliance. "'Father,' Telemachus suddenly bursts out, 'oh what a marvel fills my eyes! Look, look there—all the sides of the hall, the handsome crossbeams, pinewood rafters, the tall columns towering—all glow in my eyes like flaming fire! Surely a god is here—one of those who rule the vaulting skies!" (*Odyssey* 19.37–43).

Odysseus, aware of the dangers of fascination with numinosity, has little tolerance for his son's visionary naïveté. He roundly rebukes Telemachus for his lack of control and sends him off to bed as punishment: "Quiet! Get a grip on yourself. No more questions now. It's just the way of the gods who rule Olympus. Off you go to bed" (*Odyssey* 19.44–47).

Such a stern attitude is reminiscent of the zero tolerance in Zen

---

Pharmakon is used in Homer as both "a baneful drug and a medicinal restorative." The etymology of the word *poison* has a similarly rich shade of meaning. Through the medieval French, it is the root of both our words *potion* and *poison,* "the first poisons being love potions" (Pendell, *Pharmako Gnosis*, 3). This is much in keeping with the probable origin of the word *venom,* a love potion connected to Venus.

Buddhist monasteries toward *makyo*, those "mysterious visions" that can seduce meditation practitioners in advanced stages of practice. The standard treatment for such recurrent visions is immersion in ice water.

Nor has Odysseus much empathy for stoners, involving as the condition does loss of memory and drive in the human realm. This explains why Odysseus, that cunning raconteur with spirits, displays such ruthlessness when his crew encounters the Lotus Eaters, the island people who seduce his war-weary men by giving them the narcotic lotus to taste. Just as soldiers returning from Vietnam sought a balm for their shell shock in heroin, Odysseus's men seek merciful oblivion under the lotus' soothing effects, "all memory . . . dissolved forever" (*Odyssey* 9.109).

Harsh as a New England Puritan, Odysseus "brought them back, back to the hollow ships, and streaming tears. . . . I forced them, hauled them under the rowing benches, lashed them fast" (*Odyssey* 9.110–12).

Indeed, the mind within him that "no magic can enchant" (Odyssey 10.65), which Odysseus displays with Circe, is akin to the discerning eye toward spirits wielded by the Desert Fathers, those early Christian ascetics who fled the urban centers to seek God in the wilderness. In one account of the *Verba Senorum:*

> to one of the brethren appeared a devil, transformed into an angel of light, who said to him: I am the angel Gabriel, and I have been sent to thee. But the brother said: Think again. You must have been sent to somebody else. I haven't done anything to deserve an angel. Immediately, the devil ceased to appear.[2]

Perhaps even more in character with Odysseus's spirit, in the same text we find a tale of the unflappable Abba Macarius.

> Once Abba Macarius was traveling down from Scete to a place called Terenuthin and he went to spend the night in a pyramid where the bodies of the pagans had been laid to rest years before. And he dragged out one of the mummies and put it under his head for a pillow. The devils, seeing his boldness, flew into a rage and

decided to scare him. And they began to call out from the other bodies, as if calling to a woman: Lady, come with us to the baths. And another demon, as if he were the ghost of a woman, cried out from the body the elder was using as a pillow: This stranger is holding me down and I can't come. But the elder, far from being frightened, began to pummel the corpse, saying: Get up and go swimming if you are able. Hearing this the demons cried: You win! And they fled in confusion.[3]

Now, after following Odysseus's contest with Circe and his voyage to Hades, it is obvious that his ruthlessness toward dabblers does not arise from paranoia about altered states of consciousness. Quite the opposite. Odysseus displays a boldness of inquiry into perilous terrains of the psyche, akin to that found among indigenous medicine people. Inherent to this practice is the accrual of power, a power for which "'shamanic death' and reintegration are necessary, for they lead to a stronger mental state, enabling the shaman to negotiate more effectively with powerful spirits."[4]

Like Odysseus, with his many disguises and transformations, numbered among the "doctors" of the California Pomo and Miwok tribes were "those who dressed up in bear and panther costumes and hid out in the woods, ambushing and killing people." These ambivalent medicine men were considered doctors because of their accrued power—"because they got so good they could mimic even minor details of the behavior of the animals they 'were.' The bear doctor in the wild was virtually inseparable from the wild bear, and his claws left equivalent marks in his victim." Regarding this peculiar species of man/beast, Grossinger comments, "We see brutality and sadism—ritualized and unnecessary. They see spiritual accomplishment."[5]

In this respect we can understand Odysseus's journey home as an initiatory ordeal, sometimes deliberately undergone. It is worth reflecting on the fact that

the excruciating torture of war captives, described with righteous horror by early European observers, is identical in many of its aspects to the training of Indian physicians. Those who survived or escaped merited great medicines for their travails. They became doctors, or, if not doctors, adjudicators of rain and wind, or enchanters—for all these medicines derive from the same sources.[6]

Yet, these are extreme examples that help establish the rule. Despite the shaman's explorations of terrains and powers beyond the average human ken—or rather because of it—his or her character is often a notably attractive one. Reichel-Dolmatoff's description of the payés among the Tukano people, about whom he says, "Above all, a payé's soul should 'illuminate'; it should shine with a strong inner light rendering visible all that is in darkness, all that is hidden from ordinary knowledge and reasoning,"[7] captures the nobility, even the refined cultivation, achieved by many mature shamanic practitioners.

As we have seen with Odysseus, any survival capacity in the shamanic realm hinges on the ability to have clear and meaningful visions:

Fig. 9.1. Shaman bear effigy

"His vision must not be blurred, his sense of hearing must be acute; that is, he must be able to distinguish clearly the images that appear to his mind while in a state of trance, and to understand the supernatural voices speaking to him."[8]

But beyond these prerequisites, "what distinguishes the payé from others is that he is an intellectual."

> He is immensely curious: he is always interested in animals and plants, the weather, the stars, diseases—anything that, to others, is unpredictable. He is a humanist, in the sense that he is interested in the "pagan" antiquities of his own cultural tradition: in myths of origin, in archaeological sites, in long-forgotten place names, and in stories of legendary migrations. When a few friends gather he will talk and sing all night long. He will recall past events, speak of some special "cases" in his practice, and will be a great raconteur.[9]

Much like Odysseus, who upon encountering Dante in the *Inferno,* informs the medieval statesman that, "Men are not made to live like brutes, but to follow virtue and knowledge," the driving force for a payé is "a passionate interest in learning more and more about the powers he perceives in his vision . . . a truly intellectual interest in the unknown; and that not so much for the purpose of acquiring power over his fellow-men as for the personal satisfaction of 'knowing' things which others are unable to grasp."[10]

"Royal son of Laertes, Odysseus, master of exploits, man of pain, what now, what brings you here, forsaking the light of day?" (*Odyssey* 11.102–4), asks Tiresias when Odysseus ferrets him out in Hades.

Such discipline of mind, capacity for discrimination in expanded states of consciousness, and pragmatic, problem-solving orientation toward visionary experience clearly distinguish the experience of initiation from addiction.

As intellectually stimulating as the shamanistic quest may be, it is dangerous. It is embarked on through the body, requiring a tolerance for acute discomfort and a willingness to entertain death. An unquenchable thirst for knowledge, and a willingness to make great sacrifices for its sake, also distinguishes the shaman's character.

Hands down, the clearest dramatization of this bodily quest is the ordeal Odysseus chooses to undergo in hearing the Sirens' rapturous song. Like Kieri of the Solanaceae family, who "with the enchanting music of his violin lures the unwary and . . . whoever obeys his wiles suffers insanity or death,"[11] the song of the Sirens is so enthralling, so addictive, that Circe warns Odysseus it will "spellbind any man alive." In what can now be read as a vivid allegory for the degenerative effects of drug addiction, Circe continues, "Whoever draws too close, off guard, and catches the Sirens' voices in the air—no sailing home for him, no wife rising to meet him, no happy children beaming up at their father's face. The high, thrilling song of the Sirens will transfix him, lolling there in the meadow, round them heaps of corpses rotting away, rags of skin shriveling on their bones . . ." (*Odyssey* 12.45–52).

Circe instructs Odysseus to "stop your shipmates' ears so none can hear," yet proceeds to say, "but if *you* are bent on hearing, have them tie you hand and foot, erect at the mast-block, lashed by ropes to the mast so you can hear the Sirens' song to your heart's content" (*Odyssey* 12.55–58).

Odysseus informs his shipmates of his desire, and when, "speeding toward the Sirens' island, driven on by a brisk wind . . . the wind fell in an instant, all glazed to a dead calm, a mysterious power hushed the heaving swells" (*Odyssey* 12.181–85), they leap into action. Odysseus plugs his crewmen's ears with beeswax, and his men bind him to the mast of the ship.

Again, the episode displays compelling parallels with the experience of entering the first stage of the intensified trajectory with a psychoactive plant, or the "rush" of a smoked or injected narcotic substance, as Odysseus relates his induction into their rapturous song: "They sent their ravishing voices out across the air and the heart inside me throbbed to listen longer. I signaled the crew with frowns to set me free—they flung themselves at the oars and rowed on harder, Perimedes and Eurylochus springing up at once to bind me faster with rope upon chafing rope" (*Odyssey* 12.208–13).

Fig. 9.2. A modern vision of Odysseus's encounter with the Sirens

Their promise? "We know all the pains that the Greeks and Trojans once endured on the spreading plain of Troy when the gods willed it so—all that comes to pass on the fertile earth, we know it all!" (*Odyssey* 12.205–7). They offer anesthesia, rather than release, from the burden of memory in "the honeyed voices pouring from our lips" (*Odyssey* 12.203). Indeed, as if they have detected Odysseus's heart's desire to hear the song of his exploits at Troy sung with kleos—a desire that ultimately leads to his catharsis at the song of Demodocus—the Sirens cunningly address him with his unique epithet—*poluainos,* the "greatly praised" or "widely famous" one—aiming at the most vulnerable chink in his armor.

Odysseus's men leave him to flail in his bonds. When the island has been lost to sight over the horizon and the wind has risen again, Odysseus's crew unplug their ears of the beeswax that has preserved them and free Odysseus.

Odysseus reveals nothing of what he heard in those rapturous voices. Yet Odysseus's ordeal suggests that there is something well worth hearing in this song, something sacred even. Of such power is this maritime crucifixion that, had it been accessible to medieval allegorists, it might have been seen as a pagan foreshadowing of the Crucifixion of Christ.

Like the Gorgon head that Odysseus fears will emerge from the nethermost regions of the underworld, transfix him, and turn his psyche into stone, the Sirens embody a power dwelling deep in the psyche, which has a concealed kinship with the bards. The key difference is that bardic (and heavenly) song awakens recollection, whereas Siren song brings about narcosis, such as in Pindar's account of the golden "Charmers," creatures who perched atop a mythical temple of Apollo at Delphi and sang so sweetly that the visitors "perished there apart from wives and children, their souls suspended in the honeyed voice."[12]

In both cases, however, the hearer is, like Odysseus, bound to the mast. That is, he is transfixed within the song, and it will work its way on him. An account of St. Brendan, from the tenth century, notes that whenever music was played in his monastery, the saint would quietly insert wax plugs in his ears, which he always wore on a string around his neck. One day a talented harpist, determined to receive Brendan's blessing for his music, barged into an audience with the saint and played for him. Brendan visibly endured a performance that would have enchanted us. Perplexed, the student asked, "Why do you not listen to the music? Is it because you think it bad?"

"Not for that," said Brendan, but went on to explain. "One day when I was in this church, after Mass I was left here alone, and a great longing for my Lord seized me. As I was there, trembling and terror came upon me; I saw a shining bird at the window, and it sat on the altar. I was unable to look at it because of the rays which surrounded it, like those of the sun. 'A blessing upon you, and do you bless me, priest,' it said.

"'May God bless you,'" said Brendan. "'And who are you?'

"'The angel Michael,' the bird said, 'come to make music for you and your Lord.'

"'You are welcome to me,' said Brendan. The bird set the beak on the side of its wing, and I was listening to it from that hour to the same hour the next day; and then it bade me farewell."

Brendan scraped his stylus across the neck of the harp. "Do you think this sweet, student? I give my word before God, that after *that* music, no music of the world seems any sweeter to me than does this stylus across the neck, and to hear it I take to be but little profit."[13]

Fig. 9.3. St. Brendan not only heard heavenly music, he sailed, as did Odysseus, to islands inhabited by divinities. Here Brendan and his monks arrive at the island of Paradise, a feat that could be conceived in the sacred topography of ancient and medieval Europeans.

In a similar vein, Pablo Amaringo, the most recognized and talented of the Amazonian visionary painters, explained to us, "When you listen to the song of a spiritual being, an icaro, what a marvel!" Saying this, he pointed to one of the princely figures that inhabited the spiritual landscape of the painting unrolled on the table before us. "With this song you could live for millions of years. No desire to eat. You don't want anything, you're so content. The first time I heard an icaro, I said to my master, 'I would like to live with this for the rest of my life.' Without it wouldn't be living. The contentment, happiness, I don't know how many other things, but how, how beautiful. Those are the icaros."[14]

Much as Pindar's visitors to Delphi caught in the songs of the Charmers or in Brendan's transport in angelic music, Amaringo relates a similar total loss of appetite and state of absorption.

Plato, pointing to this underlying kinship between bardic and Siren song, states, "When the Muses first appeared to humanity, some men were so overcome with their song that they refused to eat or drink, but just sang themselves to death," apparently caught in the same labyrinth of visions as the sailors rotting away around the Sirens. He concludes, "From these maddened men came the tribe of locusts, which in like manner emerge from the ground, only to sing their seasonal song and then die"[15]

Unlike the epic bard, who *presences* the eternal inhabitants of deep time in a performance inspired by the goddess of memory, thereby countering "the decay to which mortal things are subject with a kleos [hearing that gives immortality or fame] seen as close to the very essence of life, akin to the vital fluids that sustain human life and the natural world,"[16] the song of the Sirens is a closed circuit. Like addiction, the Sirens merely entrap "the living in the putrefaction of their own hopelessly mortal remains."[17]

The pseudo-omniscient voice, the promise of intimacy in oblivion, the offer of existential release—we ought to recognize this darkly enrapturing song. We hear it in the flame hovering over the bowl of the crack pipe, the genie unloosed from the bottle, the needle plunging into the vein, the glow at the tip of the cigarette. Such Sirens leave heaps of corpses in their wake.

Gregory David Roberts, in his autobiographical novel *Shantaram*, gives us a fine simulacrum of the experience of the mariners transfixed and dying in thrall to the Sirens' voice.

Heroin is a sensory deprivation tank for the soul. Floating on the Dead Sea of the drug stone, there's no sense of pain, no regret or shame, no feelings of guilt or grief, no depression, and no desire. The sleeping universe enters and envelops every atom of existence. Thick nirvanic numbness clogs the limbs, and downward, deeper, the sleeper slides and glides toward oblivion, the perfect and eternal stone.[18]

He gives us an even better simulacrum of the experience of skirting that honeyed voice and then leaving it, as Odysseus does, in his wake. Roberts's description of going cold turkey has a remarkable symmetry with Odysseus's account of his own binding to the mast.

> Trembling and moaning with pain, I dragged the cot closer to the great window that looked out on the sea. I took up a cotton sheet and began to tear at it with my teeth. It gave way in a few places, and I ripped it along the length, tearing off strips of cloth. Frantic in my movements and close to panic, I hurled two thick, embroidered quilts onto the rope bed for a mattress, and lay down on it. Using two of the strips, I tied my ankles to the bed. With a third strip, I secured my left wrist. Then I lay down, and turned my head to look at Nazeer. I held out the remaining strip, and asked him with my eyes to bind my arm to the bed. It was the first time that we'd ever met one another's eyes in an equally honest stare.
>
> He took the strip of cloth from my hand and bound my right wrist to the frame of the bed. A shout of trapped, panic-fear escaped from my open mouth, and another. I bit down on my tongue, biting through the flesh at the sides until blood ran down my lips. He tore another thick strip from the sheet and twirled it into a corkscrew tube. Sliding it between my teeth, he tied a gag behind my head. And I bit down on the devil's tail. And I screamed.[19]

To enter into the orbit of such transfixing song, to imbibe the poison, to transmute it in the laboratory of one's own body, and to emerge newly reconstituted with enhanced survival abilities—that is Odysseus's challenge.

For Juan Flores and other native healers, whose "goal is to get back inside nature to hear her original medical voice," rather than maintaining an objective distance from their object of study, they must use their own body, as does Odysseus, as their research laboratory to "diagnose and cure illness through subjective links between themselves and nature. They present their own bodies, and they heal by the actual health emanating from their being." As in Odysseus's voluntarily undergone ordeal, "training is literally death, rebirth, empowerment."[20]

Yet an unquenchable spirit of adventure, which Dante ascribes to Odysseus in his *Inferno,* is not enough to interpret his motives. In the image of Odysseus, lashed on the mast of his ship, we see Odin hanging on the World Tree to discover the runes. Both are making sacrificial offerings of themselves.

Fig. 9.4. An ancient Greek vision of Odysseus's encounter with the Sirens

In so doing, unlike the addict, in whose trance the drug becomes his feigned ally and protector, the shaman opens himself in trance to the dream of the Earth and the night sky.

Psychologically speaking, the benefits of these kinds of initiatory ordeals, such as any spiritual practice that cracks us back open to the cosmos, are obvious. James Hillman describes how a life unleavened by dark mystery, whether from the underworld or otherworld, leads to the kind of encroaching paralysis that engenders not only depression, but addiction.

There is a curious correlation between feelings of reality about the underworld and feelings of value about the soul. It is as if, when we have no vivid imagination of the underworld, a flattening takes place, even a depersonalization that must be made good by Epicurean community and friendship—or what today is called "relating." The less underworld, the less depth, and the more horizontally spread out becomes one's life. The materialistic view ends in a kind of void, the very Halls of Hades now only a spiritual vacuum, for its myths and images have been called irrational simulacra, fantasies of fear and desire. The end is depression—and this suggests that the pervading, though masked, depression in our civilization is partly a response of the soul to its lost underworld.[21]

The final characteristic of mature shamanic practitioners is reverence. A deep respect for plants, animals, waterways, mountains, and spiritual powers, whatever their nature, is a trait found highly developed among native and traditional healers. This shows in their handling of psychoactive or addictive plants, such as tobacco.

A medicinal plant with a spirit similar in character to Hermes, tobacco is used by many of the indigenous cultures of the Americas to purify the body, set boundaries, and protect travelers, as well as direct the healing qualities of other plants. It is also the messenger par excellence, the chosen vehicle of prayers to the Creator, the breath of healing intention. So potent is the South American *Nicotiana rustica,* which packs roughly eighteen times more nicotine than its Northern cousin *Nicotiana tabacum,* that it is classified as a true psychoactive substance—there are shamans who work exclusively with tobacco.

It's something of a revelation to see how those hale old *tabaqueros,* although they smoke, eat, drink, and snort the plant, don't get cancer or display compulsive behavior in their handling of it, steering well clear of the Siren's song of addiction.

Observing these healers at work, it occurred to me that the best way for us to heal our destructive, addictive behavior toward tobacco would be to study how indigenous people use the plant as sacred medicine. That is, how to approach powerful plant spirits with reverence rather than addictive grasping.

We can also turn to the ancient Greeks, who understood the physiological process of developing tolerance to a drug's effects but had no word for addiction.* For them as well, reverence for the gifts of plants (along with recognition of their divine origins) may have been key in allowing their culture to better integrate powerful consciousness-altering and narcotic plants into their lives.

This is illustrated in a curiously forgotten episode of the myth of Prometheus, related in Apollonius's account of the voyage of Jason and the Argonauts. There we find the Titan Prometheus, cruelly bound to a mountaintop by Zeus in punishment for having brought fire and cultural knowledge to humanity, undergoing his passion—each day a great eagle descends and feasts on his liver, only to have the organ regenerate at night to begin the cycle of agony all over again.

Such is the Titan's love for humanity that even out of his torment comes a gift to relieve suffering, a plant.

> It sprang up new-formed when the flesh-tearing eagle caused bloody *ichor* from the suffering Prometheus to drip to the ground on the Caucasian crags. Its flower rises on twin stalks a cubit high; in color it resembles the Korykian crocus, and the root in the earth is like newly-cut flesh. Like the dark juice from an oak on the mountains . . .[22]

"The Greeks called the dark juice of this plant the 'drug of Prometheus,'" and it gave men strength, endurance, and resistance to pain even from weapons and fire. From a mass of supporting evidence, including the fact that "the place that Prometheus contended with Zeus was called *Mekone,* which in Greek means 'poppy,'" it is clear that Prometheus's blood, the divine ichor that runs in the veins of the immortals, "gave birth to the poppy and the poppy gave birth to painkilling opium." As D. C. A. Hillman concludes, "Prometheus enlightened mankind by giving it narcotics."[23]

Yet *narcotics* is abstract, a classificatory term, that cannot convey the nearly unfathomable reverence arising from symbiosis between plant and

---

*Thank you to D. C. A. Hillman for pointing out this curious fact to me.

human consciousness among traditional peoples. A tale of the Solanaceae family, whose vegetal genealogy has interwoven itself alongside the human throughout this work, is called for here.

I first encountered the wind in the desert, which comes as the harbinger of the tobacco spirit, as a young man. Backpacking with a friend through the state of San Luis Potosi, we had come to Real de Catorce, an old mining town fallen into ruined splendor. We wandered the deserted cobblestone streets at night, overlooked by the silhouettes of abandoned buildings outlined by the blazing stars. Below, a river ran, beyond which the desert chaparral, like an arid sea, lapped on every side. Eventually, we succumbed to the lure of that openness and shouldered our backpacks to go find peyote, a marvelous cactus of whom we'd heard tales.

After a couple days of thirsty journeying, we arrived at a stone outcropping in the desert, where we found a Huichol talisman—a rough artistic representation of the *nieríka,* or cosmic portal, into sacred reality. Singing to the peyote, we gathered the buttons and made a fire, preparing a strong tea of the plant. We then drank and settled down for the night in the desert.

That evening, as I watched the stars wheeling overhead, I attuned to the desert climate—that balance of heat, atmosphere, moisture, and mineral—as it subtly shifted and resettled into different configurations during our planet's voyage through space. At one deeply still moment, all seemed to have culminated, breathlessly awaiting. Then a wind, a gentle stirring, came and we started moving into a new day.

Toward the end of my vigil, as the coyotes began to stir, I apprehended that the passage of the night sky overhead was the archetype of all creative art, the primal inspiration in the starry mind that gave rise to poetry, mathematics, architecture, and music. Even better, it was inseparable from myself, as I sat listening to the coyotes sing in the morning. Walking out of the desert, I felt cleansed by the elements, harmonized with the chaparral, like a native son.

It was, therefore, with a mixed feeling of prodigal son homecoming and eerie bewonderment that I first heard Bob Boyll speak of that very wind I had felt stirring outside Real de Catorce in an NAC tipi meeting. It was nearing the time of the midnight smoke, when tobacco is offered in a prayer to complete the sponsor's past and move into the new life of the morning.

In that highly charged moment, Boyll gave an account of his own pilgrimage to Wiricuta, as the Huichol designate the region where Real de Catorce arose like a historical bubble on the surface of their sacred topography. He described watching his Huichol mentor, Tacho Perez, who at that time was eighty-eight years old, holding his tobacco offering at a similar hour of midnight, in watchful silence with the rest of the pilgrims camped in the desert beneath those same stars.

Finally, much as the wind of spirit, the *ruach,* came sweeping over the water when God began to create heaven and earth, Perez heard the divine wind moving high in the heavens, "crying like a baby," and was given a stick from the fire and lit his smoke.

The peyote spirit spoke to Boyll then, saying, "Watch closely. You're about to see something." Boyll blinked and saw that, with the lighting of the smoke, the shaman had been transformed. Gone was the eighty-eight-year-old Perez—across the fire sat a vital young man, wearing a cowboy hat. Much as Hermes had come to Odysseus as a "young man sporting his first beard, just in the prime and warm pride of youth" (*Odyssey* 10.307–8), the tobacco spirit had manifested through Perez as a youthful *vaquero*.

The next time I passed through that tipi flap to participate in a ceremony with the NAC, I was wearing a cast. I had punched a wall and broken my hand. Boyll, who was roadman that evening, watching me enter with Susana and our year-old daughter, Maitreya, saw that I needed a healing that night.

It was a lesson in both terror and healing. As the ceremony progressed toward the midnight smoke, a desolate isolation consumed me as the peyote medicine scoured through me. I saw a bleak future before me, where I had degenerated into an alcoholic writer recluse who would end his life alone in an insane asylum, his family lost. As midnight neared, I saw it was done. Over. The pronouncement that I would wander in darkness had been made. Even the medicine path had failed me. I was lost forever.

Fig. 9.5. Hermes

Then I heard Boyll on the other side of the tipi, addressing the sacred fire as he prepared the midnight smoke, speaking with the most exquisite humility to Creator, calling tobacco his dear friend, his companion, his way to offer an acceptable prayer that might be heard by the Highest. The earthy tones of Boyll's voice stirred a glimmer of hope in me. Bereft of any power of prayer myself, perhaps I could catch a ride on his smoke . . .

Somehow I did, and soon after a sliver of new day broke on my horizon. In the dawning light, I sat gazing into my bound hand's fracture as if it were some great rift valley, so deep I could virtually see the backs of condors riding the upwelling currents. The break wasn't in the bone at all. In punching that wall, I had manifested the rift in my own psyche from my own early family dynamics, a fracture that the Arapaho fireplace was knitting before my very eyes. Something both natural and magical was underway. The rift was closing and my psyche was taking the structure of healthy, well-formed bone again.

Before long, Susana tentatively took my hand, and our eyes met within the sacred hoop of our family. Maitreya, who had been restless all evening, satisfied herself that all was well with the father unit and the family intact. Relaxing her vigilance, she slept, until hours later I felt her little hands on my back as she, supporting herself on wobbly legs, joyfully chirruped in the morning.

Would that people acted with such reverence and gratitude for tobacco as do the native peoples who first discovered it as medicine. Would that we knew it as intimately as the Ancients once knew Hermes, guide of souls. Our veneration, I believe, would heal us of our addiction.

TEN

HEALING THE EYE
OF THE CYCLOPS

*Rescued from a dead end by the use of violent technology
more than once, man has triumphantly survived, but
remains endangered by the curse of violated nature. The
antithesis of nature and culture is more than a logical
game; it may be fatal.*

WALTER BURKERT

*You taught me your language, and my profit on't
Is I know how to curse. The red plague rid you
For learning me your language.*

CALIBAN, IN WILLIAM SHAKESPEARE'S
THE TEMPEST

In the tale of Odysseus and the Cyclops, one touches the fire-blackened
floor of the Paleolithic hunter's cave, so primordial are its elements.
Containing as it does a ritual blinding with a wooden hunting spear, a
master of animals figure, and an underlying concern with the problem of
eating and sacrifice, its provenance is clearly in the prehistoric storytelling
repertoire.

Yet the clash between the Cyclops and Odysseus is also, in its unique way, the strongest analog to a cave painting that exists in the literature of the West, containing, as it does, a sacred space where indigenous vision is transcribed for future generations.

This vision lies in its depiction of the break between the indigenous and newly emerging modern mind, one we have already seen depicted in Hopi, Incan, and other South American prophecy as the two roads of humanity: "those who know they belong to the Earth" and those who seek material, individual gain in a condition of spiritual disunity.

The tale is well known—Odysseus and his men, newly escaped from the Lotus Eaters and not yet arrived at Circe's palace, land on the shore of another unknown island, this one inhabited by a Cyclopian race. Odysseus sets out with a handful of men to explore it, to probe its resources and inhabitants. Coming on the cave of one of the natives, he makes himself at home there—over the protests of his men—and then finds himself trapped by a monstrous, one-eyed giant who scorns his demand for hospitality and starts bolting down his men for dinner. Unable to simply overpower the brute, wily Odysseus stuns the Cyclops, called Polyphemus, with powerful drink and then drills out his eye with a wooden spear, escaping the next morning with his men tied to the underbellies of the Cyclops's herd of goats.

A taunting exchange follows between Odysseus and blinded Polyphemus. When Odysseus and his men regain their ships and reach some distance from shore the prophetic nature of the blinding, and the encoded message of the indigenous oral tradition, is revealed.

As we shall see, there is good reason to interpret the Cyclops's words to Odysseus as an invitation to Odysseus to return and heal his eye—in exchange for which Polyphemus will pray to Poseidon for a blessing on his journey home. Odysseus refuses and is cursed to a vexed, long-forestalled homecoming.

Walter Burkert, a German philologist and a scholar of Greek religion, cannily identified certain key indigenous, shamanic motifs in the tale.

The first is the fire-hardened spear that Odysseus uses to gouge out the Cyclops's eye. It is simply anomalous. Why should Odysseus and his men go through such trouble to fashion Polyphemus's great club, big enough "to be the mast of a pitch-black ship with twenty oars" (*Odyssey* 9.360), into a weapon? Odysseus possesses a perfectly serviceable sword, one that he has already contemplated killing the Cyclops with. One clue is that the Cyclops's club is made of olivewood, the tree sacred to Odysseus's spirit ally, about whom he wonders, "Would Athena give me glory?" (*Odyssey* 9.355) if he strove against the Cyclops. The second is the spear, as the "the primordial weapon of man; during the Paleolithic period . . . the only effective weapon for hunting,"[1] whose ritual function continued well into the Roman and medieval worlds, is fitting to their circumstances: Odysseus and his men have been cast back into aboriginal time. While there is no documentation previous to Homer to indicate any actual historical connection to earlier ritual, it is clear that the use of fire as a way to escape danger is deeply ingrained in our species. Odysseus's fashioning of the spear on the cave floor is a magical, invocative act of the appropriate shamanic medicine to confront the cannibalistic behavior of the Cyclops.

Burkert has also shown how the Cyclops's tale parallels accounts of other violent shamanic negotiations with the master of animals to release the bounty of animals, whose souls are kept within the master's wilderness dwelling, to sustain the peoples.

Much as the Eskimo shaman triumphantly displays the blood of the mistress of animals on his harpoon, Odysseus triumphs in his goring of the Cyclops's eye.

"We find the combat myth entailed in the quest for food," Burkert notes, especially regarding Odysseus's theft of Polyphemus's flock: "This sheds light on the curious detail of the escape from the cave; in many parallels this is done by putting on sheepskins, and this masquerade may well be original. To gain the edible animals, man has to assimilate himself to them."[2]

This fact is easily confirmed by a glance at figure 10.1.

We can say with some confidence that the blinding of Polyphemus is rooted in a ritual, sacrificial act. If we widen the scope of Burkert's

Fig. 10.1. One of the famous animal-human dancing figures of Les Trois Frères cave

Fig. 10.2. Odysseus and his men blinding the Cyclops, painted on an Ancient Greek amphora

investigation, we can also detect a mythologem within its narrative, an Indo-European variation on the Expulsion from Eden motif, which preserves a memory of humankind's rupture with its indigenous roots.

As we have seen, one of the characteristics of modern consciousness is deafness to the sentience of the natural world. One of the consequences of this rupture with the cosmos is the distortion filter that lies like a dirty film over the modern capacity to accurately perceive indigenous cultures. Through this remarkable feature of perception, perfectly clear communications emerging from the natural world, including from human beings still immersed in the matrix of nature, arrive in such garbled form that they are unintelligible to the modern ear and eye, and often take on monstrous forms—as illustrated by the figure of the Cyclops.

No longer sharing in the primal experience of indigenous peoples, we literally cannot hear or see them accurately. This deafness had already emerged in the ancient Greeks, whose word for indigenous peoples, *barbaros,* meaning "foreign, strange," was onomatopoeic of the "blah blah blah" sound they heard emerging from their throats—a mimicry of the incomprehensible sound of their language, just as we use *bark* or *meow* for the vocalizations of dogs and cats. In a similar vein, indigenous peoples have often been depicted as untamed animals, much as did an early Jesuit observer of the "tribes of America," who reported, "All these barbarians have the law of wild asses—they are born, live, and die in a liberty without restraint; they do not know what is meant by bridle and bit."[3]

Yet the *Odyssey,* facing back into the prehistoric bardic repertoire as well as forward into our own time, offers us an opportunity to bridge that abyss by adopting a panoptic perspective. That is, in order to comprehend the message of the oral tradition embedded within the tale, we must learn to see through the eye of the Cyclops as well as through the eyes of Odysseus.

Odysseus, while negotiating his way through an indigenous cosmos, is also a modern in his cunning and technique. He fits the profile of the "new sort of nature traveler" poet Gary Snyder describes, who upon the exhaustion of the natural systems of Europe went forth "as resource scouts, financed by companies or aristocratic families, penetrating the lightly populated lands of people who lived in and with the wilderness. Conquistadores and priests."⁴ As well, we detect in these nature travelers, as in Shakespeare's dramatic creation of the half-man, half-monster Caliban, an "ambivalence of savagery," which simultaneously perceives a blessed innocence and arrested development in native peoples, thus requiring, as does the *Odyssey,* "the idyl as a contrasting background for cannibalism."⁵

As a mix of shaman and conquistador, Odysseus beholds the lands of the Cyclops as did many of the early invaders of the American continent, as empty wilderness, occupied by savages ignorant of land husbandry or the rudiments of civilization.

> *Lawless brutes, who trust so to the everlasting gods*
> *they never plant with their own hands or plow the soil.*
> *Unsown, unplowed, the earth teems with all they need,*
> *wheat, barley and vines, swelled by the rains of Zeus*
> *to yield a big, full-bodied wine from clustered grapes.*
> *They have no meeting place for council, no laws either,*
> *no, up on the mountain peaks they live in arching*
> > *caverns—*
> *each a law to himself, ruling his wives and children,*
> *not a care in the world for any neighbor . . .*
> *No flocks browse, no plowlands roll with wheat:*
> *unplowed, unsown forever—empty of humankind—*
> *the island just breeds droves of bleating goats. (Odyssey*
> 9.120–27, 9.135–37)

Odysseus's views have a long trajectory. Centuries later, he is echoed by figures as diverse as the Capuchin priest Gaspar de Pinell, who described the Amazon as filled with "tall trees covered with growths and funeral mosses [which] create a crypt so saddening that to the traveler it appears like walking through a tunnel of ghosts and witches. There [one is] surrounded by Indians who could at any moment kill and serve us up as tender morsels in one of their macabre feasts;"[6] or the immanent U.S. historian George Bancroft, who wrote in 1834 that before Europeans arrived North America was "an unproductive waste. Throughout its wide extent the arts had no erected monument. Its only inhabitants were a few scattered tribes of feeble barbarians, destitute of commerce and political connection. . . . In the view of civilization the immense domain was a solitude."[7]

Yet Odysseus's and his successor's reports are now being overturned as untrustworthy—on almost all fronts. In a stunning reversal of conventional thinking about the nature of indigenous interaction with the natural habitat, it has recently emerged, for example, that the Amazon rain forest is neither the ecologist's pristine, untouched expression of wild nature, nor the priest's and conquistador's howling wilderness. Giant swaths of the forest (a recent estimate is an eighth of the nonflooded Amazon forest is anthropogenic; that is, directly or indirectly created by humans)[8] could be better characterized as a great, cultivated garden, one gradually shaped over millennia by the native peoples with domesticated species of fruit-bearing trees and other plants. The oft-cited biodiversity of the Amazon rain forest is, therefore, partially attributable to the fact that we are wandering through pre-Colombian orchards!

The natives of the rain forest also discovered how to put, and keep, nutrients in the ground in a region normally characterized as "wet desert"—an ecosystem where all the nutrients are locked into the organic life of the forest and not deposited into the sandy, ancient soils. Unlike the slash-and-burn agriculture currently practiced in the Amazon (a consequence of European intrusion into the rain forest), which can only use cleared areas for a couple of seasons before the fields are leeched of nutrients, the pre-Colombian natives learned how to significantly improve their soils. Very large swaths of *terra preta do Índio*, "Indian dark earth," have recently been discovered that indicate intense cultivation of the landscape, capable of feeding millions. Such regions, unlike those under European-influenced management, are fertile even today, with "more 'plant available' phosphorus, calcium, sulfur, and nitrogen than is common in the rain forest; it also has much more organic matter, better retains moisture and nutrients, and is not rapidly exhausted by agricultural use when managed well."[9] It turns out the reports of the earliest Spanish explorers of highly developed, populous Amazonian cultures—dismissed by subsequent generations as preposterous exaggerations—may have been faithful to what the conquistadores actually beheld.

What Odysseus-minded observers have been unable to see, however, is this: the Amazon rain forest itself is one of the greatest monuments to human ingenuity and art on the planet. Abiding lightly on the earth, the pre-Colombian cultures shaped it for their uses in ways unperceived by the heavy-handed nonindigenous invaders with their Mediterranean-derived styles of agriculture. It was an Eden, in short, whose native inhabitants, as science journalist Charles Mann puts it, "rather than adapt to Nature, *created* it. They were in the midst of terraforming the Amazon when Columbus showed up and ruined everything."[10]

As well, it is generally true that indigenous cultures, far from being "lawless" with "no meeting place for council," guide themselves by custom and are less afflicted by disparities of wealth and hierarchy—what an early American colonist called the three curses of civilization: doctors, lawyers, and priests. For example, archaeology has now established that the great, indigenous ritual centers of northwestern Europe, dating back to 3500 BCE, were built without the extremes in hierarchical status and privilege that were to characterize the building of the Egyptian pyramids centuries later. Stonehenge, whose stones were transported from the Preseli Mountains of South Wales, an astonishing two hundred miles to the west, needed tens of millions of work hours to construct, yet these societies "were certainly not state societies. They are not accompanied by rich burials, nor any kind of finery. Prestige goods, such as polished stone axes of attractive materials, are not in general found associated with burials." The fact is, the archaeological record of the indigenous culture of the British Isles, whose achievements amply demonstrate "considerable managerial resources," gives no evidence of an elite ruler class. Instead, "the term 'group-oriented' is appropriate for such societies."[11]

Group oriented, with its corollary, *freedom loving,* equally applies to the Native American tribes encountered by the early colonists. "Every man is free," the frontiersman Robert Rogers told a disbelieving English audience, referring to Indian villages. In these places, he said, no other person, white or Indian, sachem or slave, has any right to deprive [anyone] of his freedom."[12] In the late 1600s, the French adventurer Louis Armand de Lom d'Arce reported how the Huron could not comprehend why

One Man should have more than another, and that the Rich should have more Respect than the Poor. . . . They brand us for Slaves, and call us miserable Souls, whose Life is not worth having, alleging, That we degrade ourselves in subjecting our selves to one Man who possesses the whole Power, and is bound by no Law but his own Will. . . . [Individual Indians] value themselves above anything that you can imagine, and this is the reason why they always give for't, *That one's as much Master as another, and since Men are all made of the same Clay there should be no Distinction or Superiority among them.*[13]

Through the eye of the Cyclops, then, we can begin to see an egalitarian culture, without the cruel refinements of hierarchy, living lightly and skillfully on the land. Adjusting for the distortion filter, in Cyclopian lifeways we can make out an echo in Odysseus's account of Hesiod's Golden Age.

They lived like gods, carefree in their hearts,
they enjoyed the delights of feasts, out of evil's reach.
The barley-giving earth asked for no toil to bring
*   forth,*
a rich and plentiful harvest. They knew no constraint
and lived in peace and abundance as lords of their
*   lands,*
Rich in flocks and dear to the blessed gods. (Hesiod
*   113–21)*

Both accounts, of course, hearken back to an age before the spread of Mediterranean-style agriculture, which for most societies was not taken up by choice any more than it was by poor Adam and Eve, whom Yahweh informed as he expelled them Eden, "Cursed is the ground for thy sake; in sorrow shalt thou eat of it all the days of thy life; Thorns also and thistles shall it bring forth to thee; and thou shalt eat the herb off the field; In the sweat of thy face shalt thou eat bread" (Genesis 3:17–19). Hunting and gathering is far less labor intensive, and studies have shown that, in general, hunter-gatherers "are healthy, suffer from little disease, enjoy a very diverse diet, and do not experience the periodic famines that befall farmers."[14]

As we have seen, they enjoy more freedom, too. Hunter-gatherer "societies tend to be relatively egalitarian, to lack full-time bureaucrats and hereditary chiefs, and to have small-scale political organization at the level of the band or tribe."[15] Farmers, on the other hand, are malnourished, vulnerable to hunger, and politically and socially repressed in comparison. Graphic evidence is given by the fact that

> paleopathologists studying ancient skeletons from Greece and Turkey found . . . the average height of hunter-gatherers in that region toward the end of the Ice Age was a generous five feet ten inches for men, five feet six inches for women. With the adoption of agriculture, height crashed, reaching by 4000 BCE a low value of only five feet three for men, five feet one for women.[16]

Odysseus, however, is blind to the virtues of such cultivated wilderness and free people. He belongs to that "healthy, nonproducing elite" whose skeletons, excavated from Greek Mycenaean tombs from 1500 BCE, demonstrate that they "enjoyed a better diet than commoners, since the royal skeletons were two or three inches taller and had better teeth."[17]

It is no surprise then, that as a resource scout, Odysseus's description of the Cyclops's so-called empty island reads like an early American prospectus for selling off ancestral Native lands to invading settlers.

> *Artisans would have made this island too*
> *a decent place to live in. . . . No mean spot,*
> *it could bear you any crop you like in season.*
> *The water-meadows along the low foaming shore*
> *run soft and moist, and your vines would never flag.*
> *The land's clear for plowing. Harvest on harvest,*
> *a man could reap a healthy stand of grain—*
> *the subsoil's dark and rich.*
> *There's a snug deep-water harbor there, what's more,*
> *no need for mooring-gear, no anchor-stones to heave,*
> *no cables to make fast. Just beach your keels, ride out*
> *the days till your shipmates' spirit stirs for open sea*
> *and a fair wind blows. And last, at the harbor's head*
> *there's a spring that rushes fresh from beneath a cave*
> *and black poplars flourish round its mouth. (Odyssey*
> *9.142–56)*

Yet wild nature still looms as a threat, as well as an investment opportunity. When Odysseus sets off to "probe the natives living over there" to discover if they are "violent, savage, lawless"* or "friendly to strangers, god-fearing men" (*Odyssey* 9.194–96), he chooses to arm himself in advance with an unusual weapon: "I took a skin of wine along, the ruddy, irresistible wine that Maron gave me once, a priest of Apollo; he lived in Apollo's holy grove. He drew it off, all unmixed—and such a bouquet, a drink fit for the gods. Whenever they'd drink the deepred mellow vintage, twenty cups of water he'd stir in one of wine and what an aroma wafted from the bowl—what magic, what a godsend!" (*Odyssey* 9.218–34).

This *magic* is "the very same Greek word used to describe the songs of the Sirens."[18] As we have already seen, Greek wine could be mixed with potent psychotropic and narcotic plants, such as opium or mandrake, and was normally mixed in a proportion of two or three parts

---

*Here Odysseus anticipates political philosopher Thomas Hobbes's view that life in nature is "solitary, poor, nasty, brutish, and short."

water to one part wine. This vintage is a cutting-edge product, a technological advance under the auspices of a god.

That this wine is from a priest of Apollo, the god whose epithets include the "road builder" and who was a special protector of colonists (as he was in the American space program), is not an accident. The Cyclops, like the indigenous peoples of the Americas, will find its intoxication a deadly foe when it is turned as a weapon against him. The stage is set, then, for a showdown between the indigenous world and those upstart new arrivals, the proto-rationalist, invading Greeks.

To return to the story, Odysseus, making his way to the Cyclops's cave, against the urging of his comrades who want to simply loot and run, builds a fire, eats the Cyclops's food, and settles down to await the creature's return in order to receive a "guest gift." When Polyphemus enters like a Tyrannosaurus Rex, however, Odysseus suddenly recalls the power of wild nature and "scuttled in panic into the deepest dark recess" of the cave with the rest of his men (*Odyssey* 9.267). There he hides until the light cast by the Cyclops's fire reveals the little men peering out fearfully.

Polyphemus immediately pegs them as soldiers of fortune out "roving the waves like pirates, sea-wolves raiding at will, who risk their lives to plunder other men" (*Odyssey* 9.286–89). Nor is Polyphemus, belonging to a more ancient culture, impressed by Odysseus's invocation of Zeus who guards guests and suppliants. "We Cyclops never blink at Zeus and Zeus's shield of storm and thunder," he grumbles, whereupon he eats a couple of Odysseus's men (*Odyssey* 9.309–10).

Things look bleak for Odysseus, rather as they did for the later conquistadores when their greed and arrogance got them in some tight spots, but Odysseus rises to the occasion when he comes forward and offers Polyphemus the wine of Apollo, "to top off the banquet of human flesh you've bolted down" (*Odyssey* 9.388–89). Polyphemus seizes the bowl and tosses it off, declaring, "Our soil yields the Cyclops powerful, fullbodied wine. . . . But this, this is nectar, ambrosia—this flows from heaven!" (*Odyssey* 9.401–3). Incredibly, the words used by Polyphemus to describe it—*nectar* and *ambrosia*—are repeated centuries later by Plato as the food given to the two horses that pull the chariot of the human soul.

After draining three fiery bowls, the Cyclops asks Odysseus's name and then topples over in a profound, drunken (or drugged) stupor.

Odysseus and his men then go to work, lighting a fire to heat the tip of the spear they so meticulously fashioned to a red-hot glow and then drilling out Polyphemus's eye, this time, curiously, with a well-developed metallurgical simile to describe the effect: "As a blacksmith plunges a glowing ax or adze in an ice-cold bath and the metal screeches steam and its temper hardens—that's the iron's strength—so the eye of the Cyclops sizzled round that stake!" (*Odyssey* 9.438–41).

It's easy for an audience to feel sympathy for Odysseus's plight and applaud his heroism here. Yet one's sympathy diminishes upon recognizing a fundamental pattern in the Homeric encounter that was to repeat itself over and over again in the spreading clash between indigenous cultures (whether hierarchical and urban like the Inca and Aztec Empires or egalitarian hunter-gatherer cultures like the North American tribes) and civilized Europeans armed with liquor, steel weaponry, deadly diseases, and abstract forms of information gathering and storage.

As with the conquistadores, Odysseus and his crew had a blend of advanced magic and technology up their sleeve that Polyphemus could not imagine. Thus we have the image of puny Odysseus with his cunning, or *mêtis*, heroically overcoming wildness. Yet while technology allows even the dullest conquistador or corporate executive to remain safe while ravaging the natural world and its inhabitants—a terrible worm in an iron cocoon—Odysseus, for all his Machiavellian cunning, is still, in the main, indigenous himself. This is what makes his capacity to use the emerging new technologies in his desperate scramble for an edge over raw nature all the more engaging and heroic.

Homer makes brilliant use of wordplay to illustrate just that point, which a Greek audience of his time, sitting around fires in stone or wood structures with wild nature pulsing just outside the boundaries of their settlements, would have deeply savored. Polyphemus, immensely pleased by the wine of Apollo, offers Odysseus a guest gift in exchange for his name. Odysseus gives him the name *ou tis*, "Nobody," a deceit that comes in useful after they've burned out his eye and the neighboring Cyclopes come to investigate Polyphemus's cries of distress, asking him, "Surely no one's rustling your flocks against your will—surely no one's trying to kill you now by fraud or force!" Polyphemus cries out, "*Ou tis,* friends. *Nobody's* killing me now by fraud and not by force!" At that, the Cyclopes shrug and say, "If you're alone, and nobody's trying to overpower you, you'd better pray to your father, Lord Poseidon," and lumber off home.

The Greek in their reply, however, has a different form for "nobody" than Polyphemus uses: it is not *ou tis,* but *mê tis,* the usual form for use after the word *if.* The linguistic wordplay lies in the fact that *mê tis,* "not anyone," happens to sound exactly the same as *mêtis,* a key word of the *Odyssey,* the main character trait of its hero—craft, cunning! "And Polyphemus is in fact being overpowered by the *mêtis,* the craft and cunning, of Odysseus."[19]

Such a narrative, while quaint and entertaining for us, would have had a much stronger resonance for the cultures of ancient Greece, who could celebrate Odysseus as a cultural hero, a bringer of the fire of technique and linguistic agility into their inheritance.

In Odysseus, then, we can see the archetype of humanity separating itself from nature, carving out the emerging individuality from the primal mind and wielding the power that comes from treating the world as an object, rather than a subject. The Cyclops, in turn, is a force of nature to be mastered, a monster, rather than a being to hold communion with. The tale is, in that sense, a celebration of "Homo sapiens, with its novel capacity and impulse to consciously plan rather than act automatically on instinct, to rely on one's own wits and will to make one's way in the world, to manipulate and control nature."[20]

Yet, as we have seen through a multitude of indigenous examples, conscious capacity to negotiate with and direct the course of wild nature does not entail a break with it. Indeed, the Celtic "passion for the wild and elemental, coupled with a gentle human love for all creation"[21] that Tolkien advanced throughout his work is only reduced to "fantasy" by rupture with a meaningful cosmos, where, "Whatever beauty and value that human beings may perceive in the universe, that universe is in itself mere matter in motion, mechanistic and purposeless, ruled by chance and necessity."[22]

Having finally seen the outcome of the potentially fatal antithesis of nature and culture, both as embodied in the oral tradition by Odysseus and in print in our daily newspapers, we can now suspect his *dolos* spirit of trickery and cunning manipulation that runs the present world. While the capacity to rely on one's wits and control nature are the very virtues for which Odysseus is celebrated, his Machiavellian objectivity has cast a deep shadow. A poisoned, species-impoverished, genetically modified earth, sea, and sky are emerging as a consequence of our break with the living pulse of nature.

Yet the oral tradition underlying the tale, which Homer imports into his account without, perhaps, recognizing its encoded message, holds out a possibility of mending this break, of achieving an integration of modern and indigenous lifeways.

Odysseus, having rustled the Cyclops's herd, boarded his ship, and put out some distance from shore, taunts the Cyclops, revealing his name: "Cyclops—if any man on the face of the earth should ask you who blinded you, shamed you so—say Odysseus, raider of cities, *he* gouged out your eye, Laertes' son who makes his home in Ithaca!" (*Odyssey* 9.558–62). Not only has Odysseus staked his claim for individual fame, but he has also, inadvertently, revealed the deeper significance of his encounter with Polyphemus, who groans back, "Oh no, no—that prophecy years ago . . . It all comes home to me with a vengeance now! . . . Telemus, Eurymus' son, a master at reading signs . . . All this, he warned me, would come to pass someday—that I'd be blinded here at the hands of one Odysseus" (*Odyssey* 9.564–70).

The indigenous Cyclops, like the Incan emperor Atahualpa two thousand years later at the hands of Francisco Pizarro and his conquistadores, could not imagine that his overthrow would happen through the clever use of technology: "I always looked for a handsome giant man to cross my path, some fighter clad in power like armor-plate, but now, look what a dwarf, a spineless good-for-nothing, stuns me with wine, then gouges out my eye!" (*Odyssey* 9.571–74).

The Cyclops then abruptly shifts his ground and begins to speak in the formulaic language of hospitality and gift exchange familiar to the rest of the *Odyssey*—he invites Odysseus to return to shore in the spirit of *xenia,* the exchange of friendship gifts and establishing relationship of host and guest. Polyphemus also offers *pompē*, a prayer to "Poseidon the earthquake god to speed you home. I am his son and he claims to be my father, true" (*Odyssey* 9.576–77).

He then reveals that Poseidon can heal his eye: "He himself will heal me if he pleases—no other blessed god, no man can do the work!" (*Odyssey* 9.578–79), but this healing somehow hinges on Odysseus's returning to shore and joining the Cyclops in this ceremonial exchange.

If we take the Cyclops's words seriously, restitution can be made on both sides, good relations established, and Odysseus can perform a healing under the auspices of Poseidon.

How this healing is to occur is not made clear, in part due to Homer's use of parataxis, where instead of supplying subordinators to weave together the meaning of the short, simple sentences the style favors, we are left with a kind of list: we must fill in the meaning ourselves.

The way the meaning has usually been supplied is this rustic Polyphemus is trying to dupe Odysseus with a transparent ploy, and when Odysseus returns to shore, the enraged Cyclops will dash out his brains on a rock. The other, far less considered interpretation is that Polyphemus is perfectly in earnest. And why should we not give the Cyclops credit? After all, Polyphemus's invitation comes hard on the heels of his recognition of the divinely woven web he has been caught in. The Cyclops now knows his guest was no mere roving sea pirate, but a person of deadly consequence, who possesses a novel power now stirring and beginning to circulate through the world.

From a mythic perspective, Odysseus represents the new upstart, the hyperactive *polymachinos,* the busy man, who is setting out in an unknown and perilous cultural direction. From an indigenous perspective, who knows what additional monstrosities may come from this cunning weakling? A blessing must be put on the hands that have gouged out the wholeness of the aboriginal eye, so that the journey of this new type of human into individuality is not alienated from its origins.

Odysseus takes the invitation seriously. He recognizes his potential instrumentality in healing the Cyclops, but his response is a curse: "Heal you! Would to god I could strip you of life and breath and ship you down to the House of Death, as surely as no one will ever heal your eyes" (*Odyssey* 9.579–82).

Enraged, the Cyclops responds with a curse of his own. He bellows out to Lord Poseidon,

> *. . . thrusting his arms to the starry skies, and prayed,*
>   *"Hear me—*
> *Poseidon, god of the sea-blue mane who rocks the earth!*
> *Come, grant that Odysseus, raider of cities,*
> *never reaches home. Or if he's fated to see*
> *his people once again and reach his well-built house*
> *and his native country, let him come home late*
> *and come a broken man—all shipmates lost*
> *alone in a stranger's ship—*
> *and let him find a world of pain at home!" (Odyssey*
>   *9.584–95)*

Here we have, then, delineated with a deft hand within this mythologem, the entire tragic history of the encounter between indigenous and modern cultures: mutual incomprehension, horrific wounding, and lingering curses. As indigenous peoples have suffered dislocation, massacre, enslavement, and wholesale genocide at the hands of European invaders and their transmitted diseases, modern culture has come home a "broken man" into the twenty-first century, racked by agonies of weapons of mass destruction, terrorist attacks, holocausts, nuclear meltdowns, an existential void leeching our bones, alone in a stranger's ship our ancestors would not recognize. We have, indeed, a world of pain at home.

Given the oral tradition's penchant for transmitting its knowledge through "lively, dynamic, often violent, characters and encounters," where its encoded information will often be cast in a fully animate form, can we not read the Cyclops's tale as addressing humanity's evolution from the same indigenous perspective as do the Hopi and Mayan prophecies?

For in the tale we have arrived at that juncture of mythic time, as in the South American prophecy of the Eagle and Condor, where humanity's paths divided, where the path of the Eagle—as represented by Odysseus, which glorifies mind, the material world, and control over nature through technology—diverges from the indigenous path of the Condor, with its connection to the Earth through ritual, spirituality, and intuition, as represented by the Cyclops.

Odysseus's refusal to heal Polyphemus's eye may preserve in dramatic form the time of discord described in Hopi prophecy, where the two roads of the prophecy stone embark from original wholeness, the upper taken by those of "two hearts," who seek material, individual gain in a condition of spiritual disunity, the lower by those of "one heart," who know they belong to the Earth.

As the Hopi prophecy depicts a bridge between the two roads that can be traversed at certain junctures, allowing those following one path to enter another, the *Odyssey* also offers a way of restitution to the enraged Poseidon.

In Hades, the prophet Tiresias offers Odysseus a curious remedy for his alienation from the Earth.

> *Carry your well-planed oar until you come*
> *to a people who know nothing of the sea,*
> *whose food is never seasoned with salt, strangers all*
> *to ships with their crimson prows and long slim oars,*
> *wings that make ships fly. And here is your sign—*
> *unmistakable, clear, so clear you cannot miss it:*
> *When another traveler falls in with you and calls*
> *that weight across your shoulder a fan to winnow grain,*
> *then plant your bladed, balanced oar in the earth*
> *and sacrifice fine beasts to the lord god of the sea . . .*
>
> *And at last your own death will steal upon you . . .*

a gentle, painless death, far from the sea it comes
to take you down, borne down with the years in ripe
*   old age*
with all your people there in blessed peace around you.
*   (Odyssey 9.139–48, 9.153–56)*

Odysseus's advanced technology was laid aside for this primal sacrifice: the blade of the oar planted in the earth irresistibly evokes the planting of a tree, the miracle of fashioned wood bursting into bloom. The sacred hoop restored, blessed peace may come upon his people and Odysseus may be carried back to his ancestral home.

"The unsettling vision of a natural self has haunted the Euro-American peoples," poet Gary Snyder has written, claiming, "there is an almost visible line that a person could walk across: out of history and into the perpetual present, a way of life attuned to the slower and steadier processes of nature. The possibility of passage into that myth-time world had been all but forgotten"[23] when the European invasion of the American continent began. Yet it may be that we are living through a greater cycle than our historical perspectives can yet encompass, one that we, like Odysseus and the Cyclops, are caught in unawares, one that we need to turn to traditional tales and indigenous prophecy to understand.

In Barry Lopez's beast fable, "Coyote and Rattlesnake,"[24] Coyote seeks out Akasitah, the creator, to demand an explanation from him for the behavior of the Shisa, those invading Euro-Americans who are making life impossible for all the other creatures on Earth.

"Below it is all chaos because of the Shisa," Coyote states. "In a while there will be no place to go. I and all my friends, even the mountains, will be taken away. How is it that the Shisa have come to this? Must I always be a coyote to the Shisa? Can I not be who I am? I ask you to change things. Let me walk out of the traps."

Akasitah tells him, "Coyote, you see like a man with only one eye. The Shisa are like a great boulder that has broken away from the side of a mountain. The boulder makes a great noise as it comes down. It tears away great chunks of earth and rock and breaks trees like twigs, throwing up a cloud of dust against the sun and you are afraid for your life. There is no need to be afraid. It only seems this way because you have never known the world without Shisa." Like us, caught in the relentless, terrifying wheel of history, Coyote needs to be reminded: "You have spent your life under the boulder."

Yet the great, roaring noise and clouds of obscuring dust arising from the Euro-American trajectory, "soon . . . will hit the earth at the bottom of the mountain and roll out into the desert leaving a little trail in the dust. The boulder will come to stop.

"You can sleep on it at night," Akasitah assures Coyote.

AFTERWORD

About the same time I began writing this book, I had a dream vision. In it I found myself in the foothills of the Sierra Nevada, with no vehicle to return the hundred miles home to San Francisco. I set out walking, thinking to myself, "The sooner commenced the sooner arrived." Before long, I come to that ideal medieval city I sometimes dream of: light-filled, cobblestoned, with soaring, intimate architecture, rounded by high walls and with waterways flowing through it. I find the gate to a school, an institute of some kind, whose halls I cannot resist entering and exploring. I glance into the classrooms, enjoy the light spilling through the large windows, observing the small groups of students engaged in concentrated work, and it occurs to me to ask about working there.

Straight away I'm given a serious hearing and am urged to apply for a workspace and a stipend to live there. I can even write my book there, I'm assured. I ask about the programs at the institute and am told there is no formal program. "Students come to learn what they need and then leave when they wish," I'm told. Touched by the freedom and openness of the institute, I walk away with the sense that I've discovered an intellectual/spiritual home. Mounting the old stone walls, I stand admiring the mythic city below me, wondering whether my family can join me at the institute, my heart soaring at the new world opening to me.

I hope this work will meet the approval of the faculty there.

A BRIEF ORIENTATION TO HOMER AND THE *ODYSSEY*

The *Odyssey* is the homecoming song, or nostos, of Odysseus, one of the warriors who fought for the Greek cause at Troy. The plot is simple enough: Odysseus, attempting to return home from victory at Troy, is doubly cursed, first for defiling the altars upon the sacking of the city, and then for blinding Polyphemus, the Cyclops son of Poseidon. Caught in the machinations of the otherworld of divinities and monsters on the wild sea for ten years, Odysseus finally escapes through the intervention of his spirit ally, Athena. The plot has three main narratives. The first, also known as the *Telemachy,* gives an account of Athena's entheogenic catalyzing of Odysseus's son, Telemachus, into manhood and his subsequent setting forth in search of his lost father. The second, the heart of the work, describes Odysseus's escape from the island of Calypso and his arrival, after suffering shipwreck, on the shore of the Phaeacians. There, having gone through catharsis hearing the songs of the bard Demodocus, he gives a nightlong bardic performance of his own, recounting his ten years lost on the ocean in the grip of Poseidon. These are the most famous, and truly ancient, of the stories of the poem: the battle with the Cyclops; the visit to the isle of Circe; the voyage to Hades, the land of the dead;

and his ordeal caught in the song of the Sirens. The third section recounts Odysseus's return to Ithaca, his reunion with his son, and the high-noon showdown in his palace with the suitors who have been plaguing his wife, Penelope, and holding his palace and lands hostage.

The *Odyssey* is actually one of two epic poems recorded by an otherwise entirely anonymous poet named Homer in the eighth century BCE* about events that had occurred in the Mycenaean world four hundred years earlier. In the first poem, the *Iliad,* which recounts the battle between the Greeks and Trojans on the plain before Troy, we encounter Odysseus, already renowned for his wiliness and stratagems. Odysseus, of course, invents the Trojan Horse, the gigantic wooden horse left at the gates of Troy as a ruse after the Greek fleet had apparently sailed for home. The interior of the sculpture, however, was filled with Greek warriors who spilled out at night, flung open the gates to the city, and brought about the violent, pitiless destruction of Troy.

Odysseus is a significant figure in the *Iliad,* but he is only one among the circle of warriors around King Agamemnon. While celebrating the arts of peace and the fragile joys of domestic life, the main interest of the *Iliad* is the loss of free will in the remorseless and tragic downward spiral of war, pervaded by the cruel indifference to human life by the cosmic order. Not only is the war initiated by events occurring on Mount Olympos, but the gods take active sides in the conflict. War is a divinely

---

*While we think of Homer as a truly ancient figure, he isn't. In many ways his historical circumstance parallels that of Sir Thomas Malory, who collected and redacted the much earlier, Celtic-inspired medieval troubadour materials on King Arthur at the close of the Middle Ages, right on the cusp of the advent of the new technology of printing. Fifteen years after his death, William Caxton's press released his *Le Mort D'Arthur.*

Similarly, Homer's epics, composed around 850 BCE, in many ways mark the close of the indigenous Greek world, recorded as they are with script. This new technology, adapted from a Phoenician syllabary around 800 BCE, made possible for the first time the notation of the vowel clusters and complex rhythms of hexameter verse. Just as Caxton's Malory concluded the Middle Ages's corpus of Arthurian literature with the new technology of printing, Homer's poems appear to have been recorded shortly after the alphabet's invention and to have marked the closing chapter of the bardic era. In fact, there is good reason to believe that Homer was both an inheritor of the ancient bardic tradition and fully literate in the modern sense.

instigated madness in the *Iliad,* which enslaves and consumes victor and vanquished alike, and as such it has its own terrible beauty, worthy of song.

Very different in nature is the *Odyssey,* which for some scholars is the more modern in individual sensibility of the two poems. Whereas Homer's account of the Trojan War has a solid core of historical truth (such a conflict did take place at Troy in the twelfth century BCE), the *Odyssey* is primarily located in sacred topography. Its most significant action takes place in sites of great, nonhuman spiritual power, deep in the wilderness of the transpersonal, oceanic realm. The poem also shows, for some scholars, a much greater feminine sensibility than the *Iliad.* Certainly, it is undeniable that Odysseus undergoes an education in his ten years of wandering, much of it at the hands of very powerful, divine females, and returns to Ithaca a man tempered, reformed of his, and the Achaean Greeks', overweening arrogance and pride.

THE PROPHECY OF THE EAGLE AND CONDOR

The prophecy of the Eagle and Condor is remarkable in that it marks the first truly international indigenous prophecy widely embraced by both Native and European-descended peoples, yet in approaching it, we need to be wary of the word *prophecy*. Anthropologist Adine Gavazzi* reminds us that prophecy in the West involves a diachronic historical process, which among the peoples of the Andes and Amazon does not exist. Rather, there is the experience of cyclical and synchronic time, where different levels of perception of reality occur simultaneously. In other words, people do not witness prophecies unfolding in the linear progression of historical time. They live and experience the reality of myth—and in postcolonial America, such revitalization of the mythic core is a potent means of cultural and political resistance.

According to anthropologist Jeff Jenkins, the prophecy of the Eagle and Condor appears in several traditional indigenous cultures of North, Central, and South America (Andean Quechua; New Mexican Hopi;

*I wish to thank Dr. Gavazzi, who specializes in the sacred architecture of Andean cultures, for her kind assistance in unraveling some of the strands out of which the Eagle and Condor prophecy is woven.

Guatemalan, Honduran, and Mexican Mayan; Ecuadorian Shuar; and others). From these different regions come prophecies with a common theme of arriving at a point when "the human family would face the choice of evolutionary transformation into symbiotic presence within the more-than-human world or to continue in the destruction of the planet."[1]

The genesis of the prophecy is shrouded. Naturally, throughout South America, the indigenous Harpy Eagle and Condor figured prominently in the cosmovisions of pre-Conquest native communities, yet there is no clear lineage of transmission for the version now in circulation.

Jenkins, inquiring into the prophecy's origin among certain elders, reports:

> What I glimpse into their understanding is that, early in their history as a people, the ways of the Condor and the ways of the Eagle were shown to them. Initially, this understanding was irrespective of north/south dichotomies. Through the generations of emergence, powerful personal, spiritual, and physical encounters clarified who the Condor was and who the Eagle was, as with any major plant, animal, mineral ally. I understand that the Condor archetype was symbiotic with the jungle Harpy Eagle archetype prior to European conquest. They soared together in both jungle and mountain terrain through the lands. The concepts of north and south and their respective archetypal and geographical resonance became clearer through subsequent centuries, when the symbol of the bald eagle became the dominating force of USA-orchestrated mass genocide of the indigenous peoples. The indigenous condor consciousness was seen as inferior. The regenerative efficiencies (harvesting carrion and bringing back the energies of the dead) of the condor's ways were disregarded. Symbolically and literally, the condor began its journey through torturous endangerment to the brink of extinction. The associations of north and south were, if I understand correctly, emergent and co-arising with the expanded intricacies of the way history panned out in the north and south.[2]

One version of the prophecy comes from Lauro Hinostroza, a Peruvian healer who now lives in Mexico City. It states that in the historical cycles of the Incan peoples at the end of the eighth *pachakuti* (each pachakuti corresponds to five hundred years), the Eagle peoples would dominate the Condor peoples for one pachakuti. This coincided with the arrival of Europeans, with their extractive economy and industries, leading to the exploitation, depopulation, and even genocidal eradication of the indigenous peoples of the Americas. The reign of the Eagle peoples was foretold to nearly bring about the extinction of the Condor peoples.

The prophecy continues with the claim that the tenth pachakuti, from the end of the twentieth century, would be a time for the peoples of the Condor and the Eagle to fly and mate together in a creative symbiosis to restore and regenerate the Earth community.[3]

One marker of this opening of the tenth pachakuti is the emerging unification of indigenous peoples and traditions, North and South, as well as the "indigenizing" of Westerners previously without a native consciousness of connection to the Earth and its larger, nonhuman community.

There are no historical documents, however, to buttress the claims of an Incan origin of this prophecy, and one hankers for a lineage. In reviewing our earliest record of Incan folklore and mythological cycles, the Huarochirí manuscript, commissioned by the Jesuit priest Francisco de Ávila in the late 1500s as part of his campaign to eradicate the power of the pre-Conquest priesthood and worship of the *huacas* among the indigenous Andean peoples, there is no trace of Hinostroza's pachakuti scheme, nor the particular eagle/condor symbolism of the prophecy.

Yet the absence of written documents does not preclude a direct lineage out of the time depths of indigenous America. Since the intercultural nature of the myth supports it being a confluence of many different indigenous prophetic streams—especially if a cross-fertilization with the Hopi and other prophetic traditions of the North, which do have a "turning point," occurred—it is probably futile to seek an original trace among surviving documents. It is through surviving *culture* that we need to gaze into the backward abyss of time.

One strong candidate for the cultural origin of the prophecy is the Taki Onkoy movement, which flourished in the latter half of the sixteenth century. This movement was widely mistaken until recent years to have been simply a short-lived political and cultural uprising against Spanish domination, until the work of Peruvian scholar Luis Millones disclosed the spiritual depths of the Taki Onkoy, including its enduring nature.

Spanish chronicles report an ecstatic dance, conducted at the huacas: sites (or loci, since humans, plants, animals, and other beings could also be huacas) in the sacred topography of the Andean people where the divine nature of the cosmos was especially manifest and accessible. There the participants underwent a process of purification, sloughing off the imposed foreign traditions cutting them off from their ancestral memory and vital connection to the indigenous cosmos, while reestablishing their communion with the huacas.

We now know that the dance of the huacas (so akin to the tragically short-lived Ghost Dance of the Northern Plains) has continued through the centuries, in disguised forms such as among the Danzantes de Tijeras, until the present. For example, in Arguedas's account of the rasu ñiti, or death dance, among the Danzantes, we see the ancestral spirit of the mountain, Wamani, appear in the form of a condor to the agonizing dancer. In this way, the dancer can die in peace, because in the trance of the dance the continuity between the past of the ancestors and the future of his surviving family and pupils is guaranteed by the presence of the condor.

Among the Ashaninca of the high rain forest, whose ancient culture displays the ability to integrate the knowledge of newcomers (as they did upon receiving many of the Incan refugees into their communities), the practice of Taki Onkoy particularly flourished. Yet it was not a mere Incan import into their culture. It rather appears both as a form of shamanistic revival that erased religious superstructures, Christian and Incan, as well as a millenaristic practice, intended to reestablish the original balance with the natural world, the spiritual ancestors and the sacred landscape through the awakening of the huacas. The messianic rebellion of the Ashaninca, led by José Santos Athahualpa in the eighteenth century in an attempt to reestablish indigenous rule in Peru, appears to have drawn much of its spiritual inspiration from the Taki Onkoy.

In the end, it is clear that the Taki Onkoy is not just a historical episode. As Lawrence Sullivan writes, "The myths and rites of the Taqui Ongo religious-dance uprising ... defy, escape or recreate their own initial historical setting in the sixteenth-century Peruvian Andes. Not only by their periodic reappearance in Andean history but also by their reappearance in ethnographies and in our own imaginations, these images transcend their original situation. Their presence among us in the twentieth century makes them and their meanings part of our own historical situation in a way that must be reckoned with."[4]

This way of ceremonial re-membering, with its messianic promise of the resurgence of native consciousness, enduring for centuries under the baleful, coercive glare of the European invaders and their predecessors, is not simply a heroic expression of a profound cosmology capable of encompassing a foreign belief system. It reminds us that the prophecy of the Eagle and Condor did not materialize out of thin air—it is a gift to us of hundreds of years of native resistance and tenacious remembering.

It is, in short, a brief lyric from a profound song of nostos.

NOTES

CHAPTER 1. THE FLIGHT OF THE EAGLE AND CONDOR

1. Devereux, *Long Trip,* 212.
2. Jenkins, *Ecozoic Neo-native Wisdom,* 10–11.
3. Snyder, *Practice of the Wild,* 42.

CHAPTER 2. SNAKE MEDICINE

1. Segal, *Singers, Heroes, and Gods in the* Odyssey, 103.
2. Jenkins, *Ecozoic Neo-native Wisdom,* 86–90.
3. Tindall, "Assessing a Quest to Heal HIV with *Vegetalista* Shamanism," 38.

CHAPTER 3. POSEIDON'S CURSE: THE RUPTURE WITH THE INDIGENOUS MIND

1. Snyder, *Practice of the Wild,* 43.
2. Merleau-Ponty, *Phenomenology of Perception,* 317.
3. McLeod and Maynor, *In the Light of Reverence.*
4. Luna, *Vegetalismo,* 73.
5. Nelson, *Make Prayers to the Raven,* 248.
6. Burkert, *Greek Religion,* 141.
7. Nelson, *Make Prayers to the Raven,* 239.
8. Ibid., 86.

9. Koch, *Bird Egg Feather Nest.*

10. Giove, *"Acerca del 'Icaro' o Canto Shamanico,"* 10.

11. Grof, *When the Impossible Happens,* 81–82.

12. Armstrong, *Short History of Myth,* 35.

13. González-Crussi, *Short History of Medicine,* 4.

14. Webster, "Some Psychological Terms in Greek Tragedy," 150.

15. Abram, *Spell of the Sensuous,* 147.

16. Nelson, *Make Prayers to the Raven,* 106.

17. Tarnas, *Cosmos and Psyche,* 80.

18. Dupré, *Passage to Modernity,* 3.

19. Ibid.

20. Lewis, *Discarded Image,* 3.

21. Dupré, *Passage to Modernity,* 3.

22. Carpenter, *Inklings,* 43.

23. Tolkien, "On Fairy Stories," 113.

24. Isaacson, *Einstein,* 549.

25. Deutscher, "Whorf Revisited," 53.

26. Ibid., 54.

27. Ibid., 55.

28. Renfrew, *Prehistory,* 176.

29. Abram, *Spell of the Sensuous,* 120–21.

30. Pendell, *Pharmako Gnosis,* 176.

CHAPTER 4. RAPTUROUS SONG

1. Amergin, "Mystery," 609.

2. Heaney, *Over Nine Waves,* 14–15.

3. This account, including the following quotes, is from Bede, *Historia Ecclesiastica Gentis Anglorum,* book IV, chapter xxiv.

4. Ibid.

5. Hesiod, *Theogony, Works and Days, Shield,* 14.

6. Tedlock, *Woman in the Shaman's Body,* 133.

7. Bustos, "House That Sings," 33.

8. Luna, *Vegetalismo,* 13.

9. Hesiod, *Theogony, Works and Days, Shield,* 15.

10. Iamblichus, "Life of Pythagoras," 72.

11. Vernant, *"Aspects mythiques de la mémoire et du temps,"* 87.

12. de Niemeyer Cesarino, *"De Duplos E Estereoscópios,"* 105–34.

13. Luna, *Vegetalismo,* 43.

14. Ibid.

15. Dodds, *Greeks and the Irrational,* 100, footnote 116.

16. Tolkien, *Lord of the Rings,* 233.

17. Flieger, *Question of Time,* 126.

18. Ibid.

19. Ibid., 193.

20. Wheelwright, *Presocratics,* 272.

21. Segal, *Singers, Heroes, and Gods in the* Odyssey, 103.

22. Bustos, "Verse of the Plant We Follow," 264.

23. Ibid.

24. Cahill, *Sailing the Wine Dark Sea,* 66.

25. Ibid., 67.

26. Segal, *Singers, Heroes, and Gods in the* Odyssey, 103.

27. Grossinger, *Planet Medicine,* 267.

28. Bustos, "Verse of the Plant We Follow," 264.

CHAPTER 5. THE PLANT GODDESS CIRCE

1. D. C. A. Hillman, *Chemical Muse,* 146.

2. Ruck, "Solving the Eleusinian Mystery," 52.

3. Pendell, *Pharmako/poeia,* 126.

4. Pendell, *Pharmako Gnosis,* 256.

5. Harpignies, *Visionary Plant Consciousness,* 134.

6. Dodds, *Greeks and the Irrational,* 73.

7. Harpignies, *Visionary Plant Consciousness,* 134.

8. Beyer, *Singing to the Plants,* 174.

9. Harpignies, *Visionary Plant Consciousness,* 149.

10. Reichel-Dolmatoff, *Shaman and the Jaguar,* xiii.

11. Furst, *Hallucinogens and Culture,* 134.

12. Ibid.

13. Askitopoulou, Ramoutsaki, and Konsolaki, "Archaeological Evidence on the Use of Opium in the Minoan World," 23.

14. Ibid., 26.

15. Ibid.

16. Ibid., 27.

17. Ibid., 25.

18. Burkert, *Greek Religion,* 172.

19. Aldhouse-Green and Aldhouse-Green, *Quest for the Shaman,* 17.

20. Burkert, *Structure and History in Greek Mythology and Ritual,* 88.

21. Reichel-Dolmatoff, *Amazonian Cosmos,* 15.

22. Ibid., 130.

23. Burkert, *Greek Religion,* 154.

24. Boer, *Homeric Hymns,* 72.

25. Reichel-Dolmatoff, *Forest Within,* 83.

26. Reichel-Dolmatoff, *Amazonian Cosmos,* 82.

27. Aldhouse-Green and Aldhouse-Green, *Quest for the Shaman,* 17.

28. Reichel-Dolmatoff, *Amazonian Cosmos,* 82.

29. Ibid., 81.

30. Ibid.

31. Luna, *Vegetalismo,* 76.

32. Luna and Amaringo, *Ayahuasca Visions,* 78.

33. Ibid.

34. Burkert, *Structure and History in Greek Mythology and Ritual,* 89

35. Bustos, "Verse of the Plant We Follow," 260.

36. Ruck, "Solving the Eleusinian Mystery," 52.

37. Luna, *Vegetalismo,* 76.

38. Ruck, "Solving the Eleusinian Mystery," 52.

39. Ibid.

40. Ibid.

41. Reichel-Dolmatoff, *Amazonian Cosmos,* 220.

42. Stein, *Persephone Unveiled,* 12.

43. Beyer, *Singing to the Plants,* 192.

44. Ibid.

45. All quotations from the *Hymn to Demeter* are from Foley, *Homeric Hymn to Demeter.*

46. Stein, *Persephone Unveiled,* 23.

47. Abram, *Spell of the Sensuous,* 120.

48. Kerenyi, *Dionysos,* 24.

49. Foley, *Homeric Hymn to Demeter,* 39.

50. Stein, *Persephone Unveiled,* 67.

51. Burkert, *Ancient Mystery Cults,* 91–92.

52. Foley, *Homeric Hymn to Demeter,* 69.

53. Ibid.

54. Tindall, *Jaguar That Roams the Mind,* 181.

CHAPTER 6. ANIMAL BECOMING

1. Schleiffer, *Sacred Narcotic Plants of the New World Indians,* 129–30.

2. Furst, *Hallucinogens and Culture,* 138.

3. Aldhouse-Green and Aldhouse-Green, *Quest for the Shaman,* 133.

4. Furst, *Hallucinogens and Culture,* 142.

5. Schultes, Hofmann, and Ratsch, *Plants of the Gods,* 110.

6. Schleiffer, *Sacred Narcotic Plants of the New World Indians,* 130–32.

7. Furst, *Hallucinogens and Culture,* 141.

8. Kroeber, *Handbook of the Indians of California,* 669–70.

9. Anonymous, *Saga of the Volsungs,* 44.

10. Sturluson, *Heimskringla,* 276.

11. Anonymous, *Mabinogi,* 96–97.

12. Ibid., 98.

13. Reichel-Dolmatoff, *San Agustín,* 92.

14. Ibid., 95.

15. Ibid., 87.

16. Fausto, "Blend of Blood and Tobacco," 163.

17. Lamb, *Rio Tigre and Beyond,* 21–24.

18. Fausto, "Blend of Blood and Tobacco," 159.

19. Ibid., 171.

20. Reichel-Dolmatoff, *San Agustín,* 87.

21. Davis, *One River,* 157.

22. Reichel-Dolmatoff, *San Agustín,* 83.

23. Ibid., 69.

24. Ibid., 70.

25. Davis, *One River,* 150.

26. Ibid., 157.

27. Lewis-Williams, *Mind in the Cave,* 209.

28. Ibid., 126.

29. Ibid., 209.

30. Ibid., 127.

31. Ibid., 128.

32. James Hillman, *Dream and the Underworld,* 26.

33. Ibid., 128–29.

34. Ibid., 129.

35. Halifax, *Shamanistic Voices,* 1.

36. Reichel-Dolmatoff, *Amazonian Cosmos,* 130.

37. Ibid.

38. Kekulé, "Benzol fest:Rede," 1302–11.

39. Narby, "Shamans and Scientists," 302.

40. Luck, "Road to Eleusis," 135–38.

41. Lewis-Williams and Pearce, *Inside the Neolithic Mind,* 70.

42. Lewis-Williams, *Mind in the Cave,* 130.

43. Ibid., 132.

44. Ibid.

CHAPTER 7. J. R. R. TOLKIEN AND THE INTENSIFIED TRAJECTORY OF CONSCIOUSNESS

1. Carpenter, *J. R. R. Tolkien,* 179.

2. Ibid., 118.

3. Flieger, *Question of Time,* 233.

4. Ibid., 246–47.

5. Ibid., 247.

6. Ibid., 249.

7. Ibid., 248–49.

8. Ibid., 250.

9. Ibid., 249.

10. Tolkien, *Lord of the Rings,* 198–99.

11. Ibid., 866.

12. Ibid.

13. Ibid.

14. Ibid., 868.

15. Ibid., 869.

16. Reichel-Dolmatoff, *Amazonian Cosmos,* 126.

17. All quotations in the following section are from Tolkien, "Smith of Wootton Major," 12–23.

18. Lewis-Williams, *Mind in the Cave,* 167.

19. Ibid.

20. Siegel and Jarvik, "Drug-Induced Hallucinations in Animals and Man," 104–5.

21. Grossinger, *Planet Medicine,* 181.

22. Ibid.

23. Neihardt, *Black Elk Speaks,* 36.

24. Ibid., 37.

25. Ibid.

26. Ibid., 38.

27. Ibid., 38–39.

28. Brown, *Bury My Heart at Wounded Knee,* 446.

CHAPTER 8. DESCENT TO HADES

1. Reichel-Dolmatoff, *Forest Within,* 164.

2. Aldhouse-Green and Aldhouse-Green, *Quest for the Shaman,* 12.

3. Dodds, *Greeks and the Irrational,* 18.

4. Beyer, *Singing to the Plants,* 166.

5. Tindall, *Jaguar That Roams the Mind,* 209.

6. Beyer, *Singing to the Plants,* 167.

7. Ibid.

8. Tindall, *The Jaguar That Roams the Mind,* 166.

9. Ibid., 167–68.

10. Quoted in Viveiros de Castro, "Perspectivism and Multinaturalism in Indigenous America," 309.

11. Lewis-Williams, *Mind in the Cave,* 209.

12. Ibid.

13. Ibid., 214.

14. Herzog, *Cave of Forgotten Dreams.*

15. Ibid.

16. Devereux, *Long Trip,* 57–58.

CHAPTER 9. BOUND TO THE MAST: INITIATION VERSUS ADDICTION

1. Pendell, *Pharmako Gnosis,* 3.
2. Merton, *Wisdom of the Desert,* 54.
3. Ibid., 57.
4. Aldhouse-Green and Aldhouse-Green, *Quest for the Shaman,* 15.
5. Grossinger, *Planet Medicine,* 86.
6. Ibid.
7. Reichel-Dolmatoff, *Shaman and the Jaguar,* 77.
8. Ibid., 107.
9. Ibid.
10. Ibid.
11. Furst, *Hallucinogens and Culture,* 134.
12. Segal, *Singers, Heroes, and Gods in the* Odyssey, 102.
13. Jackson, *Celtic Miscellany,* 282–83.
14. Tindall, *Jaguar That Roams the Mind,* 128.
15. D. C. A. Hillman, *Chemical Muse,* 178–79.
16. Segal, *Singers, Heroes, and Gods in the* Odyssey, 103.
17. Ibid., 104.
18. Roberts, *Shantaram,* 630.
19. Ibid., 651.
20. Grossinger, *Planet Medicine,* 96–97.
21. James Hillman, *Dream and the Underworld,* 73–74.
22. Apollonius, *Jason and the Golden Fleece,* 86.
23. D. C. A. Hillman, *Chemical Muse,* 101.

CHAPTER 10. HEALING THE EYE OF THE CYCLOPS

1. Burkert, *Structure and History in Greek Mythology and Ritual,* 34.
2. Ibid., 33
3. Mann, *1491,* 375.
4. Snyder, *Practice of the Wild,* 13.
5. Burkert, *Structure and History in Greek Mythology and Ritual,* 31–32.
6. Mann, *1491,* 223.
7. Bancroft, *History of the United States,* 4.
8. Mann, *1491,* 343.

9. Ibid., 345.

10. Ibid., 349.

11. Renfrew, *Prehistory,* 128.

12. Mann, *1491,* 375.

13. Ibid., 376.

14. Diamond, *Third Chimpanzee,* 184–85.

15. Diamond, *Guns, Germs, and Steel,* 89–90.

16. Diamond, *Third Chimpanzee,* 186.

17. Ibid., 188.

18. D. C. A. Hillman, *Chemical Muse,* 106.

19. See Fagles's "Notes on the Translation," in Homer, *Odyssey,* 509–10.

20. Tarnas, *Cosmos and Psyche,* 19.

21. Bamford, "Heritage of Celtic Christianity," 174.

22. Tarnas, *Cosmos and Psyche,* 17.

23. Snyder, *Practice of the Wild,* 15.

24. Lopez, *Desert Notes,* 69–70.

APPENDIX B.
THE PROPHECY OF THE EAGLE AND CONDOR

1. Jenkins, *Ecozoic Neo-native Wisdom,* 10–11.

2. Jenkins, Personal communication, 11/19/11.

3. Jenkins, *Ecozoic Neo-native Wisdom,* 10–11.

4. Sullivan, *Icanchu's Drum,* 598.

BIBLIOGRAPHY

Abram, David. *The Spell of the Sensuous: Perception and Language in a More-Than-Human World.* New York: Pantheon Books, 1996.

Aldhouse-Green, Miranda, and Stephen Aldhouse-Green. *The Quest for the Shaman.* London: Thames and Hudson, 2005.

Amergin. "The Mystery." Translated by Douglas Hyde. In *Encompassing Nature,* edited by Robert M. Torrance. Washington, D.C.: Counterpoint, 1999.

Anonymous. *The Saga of the Volsungs.* Translated by Jesse L. Byock. Berkeley: University of California Press, 1990.

Anonymous. *The Mabinogi.* Translated by Patrick K. Ford. Berkeley: University of California Press, 1977.

Apollonius of Rhodes. *Jason and the Golden Fleece.* Translated by Richard Hunter. Oxford, UK: Oxford University Press, 1998.

Armstrong, Karen. *A Short History of Myth.* New York: Canongate, 2005.

Askitopoulou, Helen, Ioanna A. Ramoutsaki, and Eleni Konsolaki. "Archaeological Evidence on the Use of Opium in the Minoan World." *International Congress,* Series 1242 (2002): 23–29.

Bamford, Christopher. "The Heritage of Celtic Christianity: Ecology and Holiness." In *The Celtic Consciousness,* edited by Robert O'Driscoll. New York: George Braziller, 1982.

Bancroft, George. *History of the United States from the Discovery of the American Continent.* Vol 1. London: George Routledge, 1854.

Bede, the Venerable. *Historia Ecclesiastica Gentis Anglorum,* Book IV, Chapter xxiv. Translated by Benjamin Slade. www.heorot.dk/bede–caedmon .html#bede-oe (accessed September 15, 2011).

Beyer, Stephan. *Singing to the Plants: A Guide to the Mestizo Shamanism in the Upper Amazon.* Albuquerque, N. Mex.: University of New Mexico Press, 2009.

Bloom, Harold. *Bloom's Guides: The* Odyssey. New York: Chelsea House, 2007.

Boer, Charles. *The Homeric Hymns.* Dallas, Tex.: Spring Publications, 1970.

Brown, Dee. *Bury My Heart at Wounded Knee.* New York: Henry Holt and Co., 1970.

Burkert, Walter. *Structure and History in Greek Mythology and Ritual.* Berkeley: University of California Press, 1979.

———. *Greek Religion.* Boston: Harvard University Press, 1985.

———. *Ancient Mystery Cults.* Boston: Harvard University Press, 1987.

Bustos, Susana. "The House That Sings: The Therapeutic Use of *Icaros* at Takiwasi." *Shaman's Drum,* no. 37 (2006): 33–39.

———. "The Verse of the Plant We Follow." In *The Jaguar That Roams the Mind,* Robert Tindall. Rochester, Vt.: Park Street Press, 2008.

Cahill, Thomas. *Sailing the Wine Dark Sea: Why the Greeks Matter.* New York: Anchor Books, 2003.

Carpenter, Humphrey. *The Inklings: C. S. Lewis, J. R. R. Tolkien, Charles Williams, and Their Friends.* Boston: Houghton Mifflin Co., 1979.

———. *J. R. R. Tolkien: A Biography.* New York: Houghton Mifflin Co., 2000.

Davis, Wade. *One River: Explorations and Discoveries in the Amazon Rainforest.* New York: Simon & Schuster Inc., 1996.

de Niemeyer Cesarino, Pedro. "*De Duplos e Estereoscópios: Paralelismo e Personificação nos Cantos Xamanísticos Ameríndios.*" *Mana* 12, no. 1 (2006): 105–34.

Deutscher, Guy. "Whorf Revisited: You Are What You Speak." In *Conformity and Conflict: Readings in Cultural Anthropology,* 14th ed. edited by James Spradley and David W. McCurdy. Upper Saddle River, N.J.: Pearson Education, 2009.

Devereux, Paul. *The Long Trip: A Prehistory of Psychedelia.* London: Penguin Books, 1997.

Diamond, Jared. *The Third Chimpanzee: The Evolution and Future of the Human Animal.* New York: HarperCollins Publishers, 1993.

———. *Guns, Germs, and Steel.* New York: Norton, 1999.

Dodds, E. R. *The Greeks and the Irrational.* Berkeley: University of California Press, 1951.

Dupré, Louis. *Passage to Modernity.* New Haven, Conn.: Yale University Press, 1993.

Dunsany, Lord. "The Hashish Man." In *At the Edge of the World,* edited by Lin Carter. New York: Ballantine Books, 1970.

Eliade, Mircea. *The Myth of the Eternal Return.* New York: Harper and Row, 1959.

Fausto, Carlos. "A Blend of Blood and Tobacco." In *Darkness and Secrecy: The Anthropology of Assault Sorcery and Witchcraft in Amazonia,* edited by Neil L. Whitehead and Robin Wright. Durham, N.C., and London: Duke University Press, 2004.

Fikes, Jay, and Jesús González Mercado. *The Man Who Ate Honey.* Taos, N. Mex.: Ambrosia Books, 2003.

Flieger, Verlyn. *A Question of Time: J. R. R. Tolkien's Road to* Faërie. Kent, Ohio: Kent State University Press, 1997.

Foley, Helene P., ed. *The Homeric Hymn to Demeter.* Princeton, N.J.: Princeton University Press, 1994.

Furst, Peter T. *Hallucinogens and Culture.* San Francisco: Chandler and Sharp Publishers, Inc., 1976.

Giove, Rosa. *"Acerca del 'Icaro' o Canto Shamanico."* Takiwasi, no. 2 (1993): 7–27.

Gogol, Nicolai V. "Ivan Fyodorovich Shponka and His Aunt." In *The Overcoat and Other Tales of Good and Evil.* Translated by David Magarshack. New York: W. W. Norton and Co., 1965.

González-Crussi, F. *A Short History of Medicine.* New York: Modern Library, 2007.

Grof, Stanislav. *The Adventure of Self Discovery.* Albany, N.Y.: State University of New York, 1988.

———. *When the Impossible Happens.* Boulder: Sounds True, Inc., 2006.

———. *LSD: Doorway to the Numinous.* Rochester, Vt.: Park Street Press, 2009.

Grossinger, Richard. *Planet Medicine: Origins.* Berkeley: North Atlantic Books, 2005.

Halifax, J. *Shamanistic Voices: A Survey of Visionary Narratives.* London: Penguin, 1979.

Harpignies, J. P. *Visionary Plant Consciousness.* Rochester, Vt.: Park Street Press, 2007.

Heaney, Marie. *Over Nine Waves.* London: Faber and Faber, 1994.

Hesiod. *Theogony, Works and Days, Shield.* Translated by Apostolos N. Athanassakis. Baltimore, Md.: Johns Hopkins University Press, 1983.

Herzog, Werner. *Cave of Forgotten Dreams.* IFC Films, 2010.

Hillman, D. C. A. *The Chemical Muse.* New York: St. Martin's Press, 2008.

Hillman, James. *The Dream and the Underworld*. New York: Harper and Row, 1979.

Homer. *The Odyssey*. Translated by Robert Fagles. New York: Penguin Books, 1996.

Iamblichus of Chalcis. "The Life of Pythagoras." In *The Pythagorean Sourcebook and Library*. Translated by Kenneth Guthrie. Grand Rapids, Mich.: Phanes Press, 1987.

Isaacson, Walter. *Einstein: His Life and Universe*. New York: Simon & Schuster, 2007.

Jackson, Kenneth. *A Celtic Miscellany*. New York: Penguin Books, 1951.

Jenkins, Jeff. *An Ecozoic Neo-native Wisdom: Interfacing Cosmological Indigenous Ritual and the Story of the Universe*. Ph.D. diss. California Institute for Integral Studies, 2012.

———. Personal communication, November 19, 2011

Kekulé, F. A. "Benzolfest: Rede." In *Berichte der Deutschen Chemischen Gesellschaft* 23 (1890): 1302–11.

Kerenyi, Karl. *Dionysos: Archetypal Image of Indestructible Life*. Princeton, N.J.: Princeton University Press, 1976.

Koch, Maryjo. *Bird Egg Feather Nest*. New York: Stewart, Tabori, and Chang, 1992.

Kroeber, Alfred L. *Handbook of the Indians of California*. Berkeley: California Book Co., 1953.

Lamb, Bruce. *Rio Tigre and Beyond: The Amazon Jungle Medicine of Manuel Córdova*. Berkeley: North Atlantic Books, 1985.

Lewis, C. S. *The Discarded Image: An Introduction to Medieval and Renaissance Literature*. Cambridge, UK: Cambridge University Press, 1964.

Lewis-Williams, David. *The Mind in the Cave*. London: Thames and Hudson, 2002.

Lewis-Williams, David, and David Pearce. *Inside the Neolithic Mind*. London: Thames and Hudson, 2005.

Lopez, Barry Holstun. *Desert Notes: Reflections in the Eye of a Raven*. New York: Avon Books, 1981.

Luck, G. "The Road to Eleusis." *American Journal of Philology* 122, no. 1 (2001): 135–38.

Luna, Luis Eduardo. *Vegetalismo: Shamanism among the Mestizo Population of the Peruvian Amazon*. Stockholm, Sweden: Stockholm Studies in Comparative Religion, 1986.

Luna, Luis Eduardo, and Pablo Amaringo. *Ayahuasca Visions*. Berkeley: North Atlantic Press, 1999.

Mann, Charles C. *1491: New Revelations of the Americas before Columbus*. New York: Vintage Books, 2006.

McLeod, Christopher, and Malinda Maynor. *In the Light of Reverence*. Bullfrog Films, 2001.

Merleau-Ponty, M. *The Phenomenology of Perception*. Translated by Colin Smith. London: Routledge and Kegan Paul, 1970.

Merton, Thomas. *The Wisdom of the Desert: Sayings from the Desert Fathers of the Fourth Century*. New York: New Directions Books, 1970.

Nagy, Gregory. "Comparative Studies in Greek and Indic Meter." *Harvard Studies in Comparative Literature* 33 (1974): xxii, 335.

Narby, Jeremy. *The Cosmic Serpent*. New York: Penguin Putnam, 1998.

———. "Shamans and Scientists." In *Shamans through Time: 500 Years on the Path to Knowledge*, edited by Jeremy Narby and Francis Huxley. New York: Jeremy P. Tarcher/Putnam, 2001.

———. "Interview Jeremy Narby, part 3 of 4." In *A General Introduction to Ayahuasca*, October 2007. www.ayahuasca-info.com/interview_jeremy_narby_3 (accessed April 10, 2011).

Neihardt, John. *Black Elk Speaks*. Lincoln, Nebr.: University of Nebraska Press, 1995.

Nelson, Richard K. *Make Prayers to the Raven: A Koyukan View of the Northern Forest*. Chicago: University of Chicago Press, 1983.

Pendell, Dale. *Pharmako/poeia*. San Francisco: Mercury House, 1995.

———. *Pharmako Gnosis*. San Francisco: Mercury House, 2005.

Perkins, John. *The World Is As You Dream It: Teachings from the Amazon and Andes*. Rochester, Vt.: Destiny Books, 1994.

———. *Shapeshifting: Shamanic Techniques for Global and Personal Transformation*. Rochester, Vt.: Destiny Books, 1997.

Perkins, John, and Shakaim Mariano Shakai Ijisam Chumpi. *Spirit of the Shuar: Wisdom from the Last Unconquered People of the Amazon*. Rochester, Vt.: Destiny Books, 2001.

Reichel-Dolmatoff, Gerardo. *Amazonian Cosmos: The Sexual and Religious Symbolism of the Tukano Indians*. Chicago: University of Chicago Press, 1971.

———. *San Agustín: A Culture of Colombia*. New York: Praeger Publishers, 1972.

———. *The Shaman and the Jaguar: A Study of Narcotic Drugs among the Indians of Colombia*. Philadelphia, Pa.: Temple University Press, 1975.

———. *The Forest Within: The World-View of the Tukano Amazonian Indians*. Devonshire, UK: Themis Books, 1996.

Renfrew, Colin. *Prehistory: The Making of the Human Mind*. New York: The Modern Library, 2009.

Roberts, Gregory David. *Shantaram*. New York: St. Martin's Press, 2003.

Ruck, Carl A. "Solving the Eleusinian Mystery." In *The Road to Eleusis*, edited by Robert Forte. Berkeley: North Atlantic Books, 2008.

Ruck, Carl A., and Danny Staples. *The World of Classical Myth*. Durham, N.C.: Carolina Academic Press, 1994.

Schleiffer, Hedwig. *Sacred Narcotic Plants of the New World Indians: An Anthology of Texts from the Sixteenth Century to Date*. New York: Hafner, 1973.

Schultes, Richard Evans, Albert Hofmann, and Christian Ratsch. *Plants of the Gods*. Rochester, Vt.: Healing Arts Press, 2001.

Segal, Charles. *Singers, Heroes, and Gods in The* Odyssey. New York: Cornell University Press, 1994.

Shakespeare, William. *The Complete Works of Shakespeare,* edited by David Bevington. New York: Longman, 1997.

Siegel, Ronald, and M. E. Jarvik. "Drug-Induced Hallucinations in Animals and Man." In *Hallucinations: Behavior, Experience, and Theory*, edited by R. K. Siegel and L. J. West. New York: John Wiley, 1975.

Sjoestedt, Marie-Louise. *Gods and Heroes of the Celts*. Translated by Myles Dillon. Berkeley: Turtle Island Foundation, 1982.

Snyder, Gary. *The Practice of the Wild*. Washington, D.C.: Shoemaker and Hoard, 2004.

Stein, Charles. *Persephone Unveiled*. Berkeley: North Atlantic Books, 2006.

Sturluson, Snorri. *The Heimskringla*. Translated by Samuel Laing. London: John C. Nimmo, 1889.

Sullivan, Lawrence E. *Icanchu's Drum: An Orientation to Meaning in South American Religions*. New York: Macmillan Co., 1988.

Tarnas, Richard. *Cosmos and Psyche*. New York: Viking, 2006.

Tedlock, Barbara. *The Woman in the Shaman's Body*. New York: Bantam Books, 2005.

Tindall, Robert. *The Jaguar That Roams the Mind*. Rochester, Vt.: Park Street Press, 2008.

———. "Assessing a Quest to Heal HIV with *Vegetalista* Shamanism." *ReVision* 32, no. 2 (Fall 2010): 38–43.

Tolkien, J. R. R. "On Fairy Stories." In *A Tolkien Miscellany*. New York: Quality Paperback Book Club, 2002.

———. "Smith of Wootton Major." In *A Tolkien Miscellany*. New York: Quality Paperback Book Club, 2002.

———. *The Lord of the Rings*. New York: Houghton Mifflin Company, 2004.

Vernant, Jean-Pierre. *"Aspects mythiques de la mémoire et du temps."* In *Mythe et pensée chez les grecs* 3rd ed. Paris: F. Maspero, 1974.

Viveiros de Castro, E. B. "Perspectivism and Multinaturalism in Indigenous America." In *The Land Within: Indigenous Territory and the Perception of the Environment,* edited by A. Surrallés and P. García Hierro. Copenhagen: International Work Group for Indigenous Affairs, 2005.

Wasson, Gordon R., Albert Hofmann, and Carl A. P. Ruck. *The Road to Eleusis,* edited by Robert Forte, Berkeley: North Point Press, 2008.

Webster, T. B. L. "Some Psychological Terms in Greek Tragedy." *Journal of Hellenic Studies* 77 (1957): 149–54.

Wheelwright, Philip, ed. *The Presocratics*. Indianapolis, Ind.: Odyssey Press, 1966.

INDEX

Page numbers in *italics* represent illustrations.